STARTING

the Western

HORSE

ALSO BY J.P. FORGET

The Complete Guide to Western Horsemanship

STARTING
the Western
HORSE

A Guide to Preparing the Green Horse
for Optimum Performance
Under Saddle

J.P. FORGET

Howell Book House
NEW YORK

To all my students, for what you have taught me.

All photographs by Louise Forget unless otherwise noted
Line drawings by Patricia Simoneau

Howell Book House
A Simon & Schuster Macmillan Company
1633 Broadway
New York, NY 10019

MACMILLAN is a registered trademark of Macmillan, Inc.

Library of Congress Cataloging-in-Publication Data

Forget, J. P.
   Starting the western horse : a guide to preparing the green horse for optimum performance under saddle /
J.P. Forget
       p.   cm.
   Includes index.
   ISBN: 0-87605-926-4
   1. Western horses—Training.   2. Western riding.   I. Title.
SF309.34.F67 1997   96-33104
636.1'088—dc20   CIP
Manufactured in the United States of America
10 9 8 7 6 5 4 3 2 1

CONTENTS

ACKNOWLEDGMENTS

I thank the following people for their support and help:

Louise Forget, Daniel Forget, Alberta and Cecile Forget, Greg Lajoie, Wayne Latimer, Randy Paul, Doug Milholland, Kevin Pole, Locke and Deb Duce, Peter Campbell, Roger Thomason, Lisa Carlson, Tori Bedford, Tracy MacIntyre, Roland Sawatsky, Jim Kubiak, Denis Kennedy, Lorne and Ethel Sharkey, Sigmund Brower, Doug Petersen, Les McKenzie, Maxine Rusnak, Lori Carifelle, and Pernell Fleck.

FOREWORD

How a colt is started has a bearing on his performance potential. For in order to achieve his maximum performance, a colt must have been started in a way that leads him to become a willing partner with the human from the very beginning.

J.P. Forget has put together a system that does just that. And this book about his system is one that should be read again and again. It outlines simple but key concepts that lead a colt to want to partner-up with the handler. It details exercises you can use to bring your colt to willingly participate in his schooling. At the same time as these exercises work on your colt's mind, they prepare his body for maximum and perhaps unparalleled performance.

Throughout the book you can read about the signs to watch for when starting a colt. These signs are critical to developing a positive relationship with your colt. The objectives of the first thirty rides are very well described and the book tells exactly what to do and what to expect.

Starting the Western Horse is a necessary addition to the library of anyone seriously interested in the art of starting colts.

Congratulations, J.P.! Thousands will experience new levels of personal achievement with their colts as a result of your book!

DICK PIEPER
NRHA past president
NRHA Hall of Fame inductee

INTRODUCTION

"T is the good reader that makes the book," said Ralph Waldo Emerson. There is no book that proves this statement more true than *Starting the Western Horse*, which was written for those who have a sense of always doing things better. This book is for horsemen and horsewomen who want to develop a deeper, more successful relationship with their horses. It is for horse trainers who want to save themselves and their horses time and achieve a higher level of accomplishment in the process. While some good will come from reading this book, those who diligently, persistently, and creatively apply the principles outlined in its pages will reap greater benefits, both personally and professionally.

Starting colts is not something that came easily to me. Rather, it is through having started over 1,200 head of colts of several different mental dispositions that I have come to learn the approaches described in this book. It is through teaching others to start at least that many more that I learned to relate the steps involved. I have applied all types of approaches to starting all types of horses, some with greater results than others. For these reasons, I feel well qualified to teach you these skills.

PREPARATION

Preparation is the doorway to performance. A horse that is prepared for a transition into the lope departs in a relaxed, balanced, refined way. One that is not rushes into it, often picking up the wrong lead as he pushes against the rider's aids. A horse that is prepared for the stop performs with his hind legs under him; he is relaxed in the front limbs and does not push his head up or open his mouth.

A horse that is prepared for cutting a cow is attentive to the cattle in front of him—ready to dash to the left or to the right according to the cow's movement, all of it on a loose rein, confident that he is at the right place to work the cow and maintain control. The cutting horse that is not prepared will make a few moves, but the pressure of not knowing he is ready and able to keep his working advantage will get to him. Often this horse will get up on his hind legs and walk away from the cut, head up high and scared, thinking only, "Let me out of here."

The well-prepared barrel horse makes a tight turn around each barrel. The poorly prepared barrel racer likely will go wide, losing precious seconds around the first barrel because the rider does not have the control she needs. The horse's shoulder will lean into the second and third barrel, forcing him wide in the pocket and making him lose more time and money.

The poorly prepared family horse is difficult to catch, often pulls back on the halter when tied safely, sometimes refuses to walk away from the barn, and perhaps even bucks as the rider calls for the trot or lope.

This book is about preparing the colt for optimum performance regardless of the event in which you wish to participate. It is about building a relationship with your colt as you go through the process of working under saddle the first few times. It is about working with your colt's mind toward a state of relaxation and cooperation within which the colt does things because it is his idea to do them.

How one should start a colt is not necessarily cut and dried. You will not know what to do until you approach the colt. At this point he will tell you what he needs and what adjustments you have to make for the two of you to work together as a team. Therefore be careful not to think of this book as a recipe book: mix the ingredients in the right order, place in the oven at a specific temperature for a set period of time, and the cake will certainly be a success. In horse training you have to adjust to fit the situation. Rarely if ever will you add the same mix of ingredients in the same order at the same time. Every colt is different, and everything you do must be adjusted according to the background, disposition, and athletic ability of the individual horse. The more colts you start, the more experience you will have and the more certain you will feel about the adjustments you will make.

The exercises or ingredients listed in this book form a frame of reference that you can adapt to the colts you are working with. For instance, a colt that responds to the flag quietly and begins to bend immediately may not need as much work as one that is tight and scared and "freezes" when he sees the flag. A colt that has never had a halter on and stands away from you needs to start at a different point than a barn-raised colt you have made friends with from the day he was born.

Regardless of your colt's background, the method of starting colts explained in this book results in a very quiet, tranquil horse—one that is comfortable in his environment and does the things you ask because all along you have been partners rather than enemies.

This method also speeds up the training process. Although it may seem like you are doing an enormous amount of groundwork, it will progress very quickly if you do the right things, and soon the colt will be going under saddle. However, the real advance in the training process takes place in the colt's mind when you start him using this method. As you gain and direct his attention, his body becomes better prepared for such activities as cutting, roping, reining, and western pleasure.

NEW BITTING METHOD

In this book I introduce a most effective, horse-centered approach to bitting the green colt: the relaxation method. The relaxation method is the most effective way of introducing a colt to the desired response to bit pressure. In fact, it is so effective that the training program is advanced by several days, or even weeks and perhaps months, by using this method. The reason for this is best described by its name: relaxation. The method provides the colt with the opportunity to learn the desired responses without experiencing the fear and pain, and attempting the escapes, that result from other methods of bitting.

Regardless of other methods you may choose, only this one will provide you with the opportunity to feel your colt's mouth during this critical development stage. None of the other methods will bring about such profound muscular suppleness and strength that this method will. No other bitting method will let you into your horse's mind as well as the relaxation method. For this method to work, however, you must be attentive to the signs your colt sends your way as you apply the program. You must not approach this method as a recipe that you simply make your way through.

INDEPENDENT SEAT

There is a key you must possess if this method of starting colts is to work for you and your colts to the fullest. This key is an independent seat. Unless a rider possesses all the qualities of an independent seat, she will not be able to bring a colt to his maximum level of performance. One who does not have an independent seat can do the groundwork, but mounting the colt and riding effectively will be impossible without it.

This is because a rider who has an independent seat can maintain—without conscious effort—stability of the upper body, suppleness of the midsection, adherence of the thighs, stability of the legs without rigidity, and ease of movement in the shoulders, neck, and arms. These characteristics lead to an ability to apply any aid or combination of aids without loss of balance or unwanted application of unnecessary cues; your body is completely steady, and you are able to counterbalance any action or jolt the colt may send your way.

A lack of independent seat is very often the reason a colt spooks and jolts the rider. It's like the proverbial vicious circle. The rider loses balance slightly, and the colt is drawn out of balance. Because he is out of balance, the colt speeds up or jolts himself in the opposite direction to regain his balance. The rider, already out of balance, tenses up and squeezes the legs to stay with the colt. The colt, in addition to being out of balance, is now scared by the abrupt, unusual and threatening actions the rider is now taking. He jumps ahead. The focus is no longer on regaining balance but rather on escaping the threatening environment he suddenly finds himself in. The rider completely loses balance and falls. Possibly injured, the rider may now fear mounting the colt, who now associates a rider on his back with danger.

Situations like these happen all too often because a rider has not invested the time necessary to develop an independent seat. With an independent seat, a rider avoids putting the colt out of balance to begin with. When the colt gets out of balance—and he will since he is not accustomed to carrying a rider—the rider with the independent seat is able to use her body and her seat to bring the colt back into balance rather than contributing to the problem.

Achieving an independent seat is a challenging and exciting process. It is described in detail in *The Complete Guide To Western Horsemanship* by this author and published by Howell Book House.

Before we get into starting your colt, remember that your safety is always first. Do not talk yourself into a situation that you cannot handle or do not have the experience to assess and rectify. Your colt's safety is a close second. Be sure that everything you do is safe for the colt, from the saddle you use to the place where you tie him for grooming.

And finally, enjoy the process. If this is not going to be fun for you, it is not worth your doing it.

I

THE PHILOSOPHICAL FOUNDATION

Before I discuss the philosophical foundation of schooling the colt, it is important to address some critical principles of human behavior with regard to horses. First, it must be a personal goal of the trainer to better herself, not to better the horse. Schooling a colt is first and foremost not dominating the horse, but rather dominating oneself. In this book, I refer to schooling the colt as an opportunity to develop a team relationship with your animal. On a team there must be a leader. The leader, to be effective, must be able to control her emotions. That is not to say she may not have emotions, but rather that in order to lead she must be in control of her emotions and actions.

Since every aspect of your personality affects training, and balance is key to successful teamwork, in order to be the leader of this team that you are about to develop, you must improve all aspects of your personality. For instance, failure to develop a keen sense of observation will not necessarily be made up for by a great ability to sit quietly.

Recognizing that the colt is always right leads to the kind of result Olds Little Rebel exhibits in this action shot: lightning fast, flat spins, on loose reins. Turns such as these mark high in reining and working cow horse events.

"THE COLT IS ALWAYS RIGHT"

A key principle to remember as you work with your colt is this: When the colt is not doing what you want him to do, he is not trying to get the best of you. He just does not recognize what you are asking for. He has no choice. In not responding, he is sending a message: "I am confused. I am not trying to insult you. I simply do not understand what you want me to do." The way you present the request is unclear to him. The famous horseman Tom Dorrance says: "I will be the horse's lawyer, and I will win every time because the horse is always right." Indeed, the colt is always right. If things are not happening the way you think they should, ask yourself what it is that you are not doing right. Somehow your colt sent you a message a while back that you did not recognize or heed. Go back and decode that message; comply with the necessary steps the colt is telling you to follow; and things will begin to progress again.

MAKING EXCUSES

Do you feel a small amount of improvement in your horse's performance every day you school him? One of the traps we often fall into is making excuses for our horses. We ride them or work with them with the idea that the colt is only a three-year-old and therefore should not be expected to neck rein, or that we should not be asking a two-year-old for a lateral movement such as pivot-on-the-forehand.

When I give seminars on horse training or horsemanship, I very often begin by asking each participant to tell me about the horse he or she is riding. At one particular seminar, I listened as a rider told me that the horse she was sitting on was twelve or so years old. As I looked at the horse I noticed the snaffle bit in his mouth. "Have you ever ridden him with one hand and one finger between the reins?" I asked. " No," came the reply, "he is still very green."

For the best part of ten years this rider had made excuses for her horse, reasoning why he would not be ready to perform at a more advanced level. She did not realize until she began to work with her horse and applied some of the approaches I taught at the seminar that she had greatly limited her horsemanship experience by not expecting a small increase in performance every time she worked her horse. She did not know the horse could respond because she never asked. Instead, she assumed he could not do it and thus limited his and her accomplishments.

At another seminar, one woman counted the excuses riders came up with as they discussed their horses' performance under saddle. By the end of the first day, she had documented twenty-three various excuses offered by the fourteen participants in the seminar!

Ask yourself if you make up excuses for your horses. You may find yourself saying things like "He is too young," "He can't bend to the left," "He is not very agile," "He is too old," "He does not want to do this. . . . "

ASK FOR LITTLE, REWARD FOR LESS

On the other hand, there is such a thing as expecting too much of a horse. A horse bred for western pleasure is not going to give the same performance on the racetrack as one that is bred to run. However, here we are talking performance level, not schooling levels. There is no real reason why both horses cannot learn the schooling principles of guiding on the circle or moving away from leg pressure at practically the same rate. I say "practically" because every horse is different and some do handle training better and more willingly than others. Barring the difference of a few days or weeks, both horses should learn to respond to the aids in the desired fashion.

In this book, I will take you through the steps involved in starting a colt. As you apply the steps, keep in mind that training will progress faster if you ask for little and reward as you get less. You are right. You did read *reward as you get less.* There are two reasons for this:

1. Asking for little, you have a much better chance of getting it than if you ask for much. Hence, you build responses in your colt.

2. Rewarding as you get less allows you to show your colt that it was even easier than anticipated and that the reward came as he performed, not after.

In other words, the reward comes to the colt as soon as he makes an effort toward the goal.

"Let's Do This, Please"

The way you communicate with your horse has a great bearing on how he responds to the aids. When you say "Whoa" and pick up on the reins to stop your horse, does he root his nose out, stick his front legs in the ground, jar you as he stops? If so, you are saying, "Do this now," rather than the much more effective, "Let's do this, please."

The "do this now" approach of intimidation causes fear in the horse. In an attempt to protect himself from what he perceives as an insecure environment, the colt begins to brace. This bracing results in a tightening of the muscles and an inability to move freely in response to your aids. As the colt tightens you say even louder, "Do this now," and a vicious cycle begins. The colt braces even more, making him even less able to respond to the bit and other cues you are giving him. Finally, the mental pressure builds to the point where the colt fears for his life and will attempt escape by any means possible. If you are working on the ground, this usually means that the colt will pull away. If he is tied to a fence, he is likely to pull back or try to jump it. If you are riding him when you

What better than to ride a horse that is always prepared to say, "Yes, sir/ma'am" because to him, everything you ask has become a pleasant pastime. Author partners up with Olds Little Rebel for a dramatic sliding stop. Photo: Janet Rose.

give the "Do this now" command, he will respond with abrupt, jumpy moves rather than the smooth, controlled, and willing moves characteristic of the advanced performances of winning rider/horse teams.

The key to optimum performance is to apply your aids in a calm, slow, and soft fashion. These include all the aids you use, from the flag as you begin the desensitization process, all the way up to the hands and legs on the advanced horse. "You offer it to him in a good way," says Ray Hunt as he speaks of this approach to applying the aids. The long-term results are well worth the effort required to focus on this way of applying the aids: a willing, relaxed horse that performs smoothly with control but as fast as you want. What is better than to ride a horse that is always prepared to say, "Yes sir/ma'am" because to him, everything you ask has become a pleasant pastime?

The Right Thing is More Comfortable Than the Wrong Thing

An important aspect of this method of starting a colt is to make the right thing more comfortable than the wrong thing. In all the exercises you experience with your colt, be sure that the desired response is more comfortable for him than any of the other responses. Soon your colt will respond because it is his idea, not yours.

For instance, this method of starting a colt does not advocate the use of hobbles. You want the colt to know that he can move away if he wants to. He is not trapped. You simply make it easier for him to stand there than to be far away. Standing there becomes the colt's idea. Since you are not forcing him to stand still by tying him or using hobbles, progress will take place at a faster pace, and a relationship of trust will be established.

Reward Small Changes in Behavior

Rewarding minute changes in behavior is another fundamental principle of this approach to training. Rewarding the small changes means that you are watching for signs of change and that you recognize them when the colt thinks about a change. Signs may include but are not limited to licking the lips, wanting to stop and stand still, lowering the neck, slowing down, moving at a consistent pace, etc.

There is a multiplicity of signs you need to be aware of as you work with horses, particularly colts. Throughout the book I will point out the signs you need to look for at specific stages of the training process. Observing even the smallest of signs and rewarding them builds the colt's confidence in you as a safe element of his environment and further contributes to his relaxation. If in doubt as to whether a response was right or wrong, give the colt the benefit of the doubt. As a result, training will progress at a faster pace and with less stress and effort on both your parts.

Turning Bad into Good

In this method of starting colts you will learn to turn natural barriers into positive forces for change and optimum performance. One of the ways in which you will turn bad into good is by using the colt's natural fears to achieve suppleness, strength, and ability to engage the hindquarters and step laterally with the forequarters. This will take place during the flagging and suppling process.

Another way to turn bad into good is to let the colt walk on when he breaks gait or tentatively moves forward for one or two steps, then stops. Rather than bump him forward and scare him, turn the break of gait into an opportunity for him to learn to slow down and relax.

Apply the above principles as you work your way through the steps outlined in this book and you will find your colt learning faster and performing better.

2

EQUIPMENT

Schooling horses, like any other sophisticated activity, calls for the right tools for the job. It is hard to imagine wanting to haul your horse somewhere if the mechanic who tuned your truck did it without the use of a computerized scope. Yet many times we attempt to achieve professional results without the proper tools. In this chapter I will discuss the tools you need to start colts effectively and safely, focusing on the basic, safe, working tools.

WORKING AREA (PEN)

The working area may consist of two pens: a round pen approximately 60 feet in diameter, and a small round or square pen approximately 15 feet across. The small pen will be used for mounting the colt for the first few rides or until you feel safe to ride him in a bigger pen. The larger round pen is the pen you will progress to after you have ridden in the smaller pen. Both pens should be connected by a gate to save on walking and time. For the same reasons, they should be located close to your stabling area. Well-designed facilities usually have no more than the width of a driveway between the stable and the round pens.

The fence should be 6 to 7 feet high. This is not necessarily to prevent the colts from jumping the fence, although with some colts this may be a concern. Rather, the purpose of the high fence is to help keep the colt focused on you as you work with him. Training will progress faster if the colt is not distracted by outside attractions at the beginning. The bottom 4 feet of the fence should be solid to prevent the colt from slipping a leg between the bottom rails and injuring himself.

The ground surface should be soft. Four inches of fine washed sand is ideal. Ground that is deeper than 4 inches is very hard on a horse's tendons and may cause soft tissue injuries. Shallow, hard ground causes severe impacting on the colt's limbs as he moves about and eventually causes joint and bone injuries.

The ground surface will need to be dragged with harrows regularly to keep it spongy and level. Therefore, the gate to the larger round pen must be wide enough to let a tractor through.

The entire area must be safe and clear of any sharp objects, ropes, or wire hanging from the fence. Keep the ground free of implements or anything else that could quickly become traps for the colt and rider and result in injuries. At least one post of your larger pen should be solid enough to tie a colt to. I am not referring here to a snubbing post since this method of starting a colt does not advocate snubbing. Nevertheless, you will need a post sufficiently solid to hold a colt as you work on desensitizing him. If your larger pen is built of wood, it is likely that any post is solid enough for the purpose. If it is built of portable panels, as many are, you will need to drive a post in the ground right next to the fence on the outside of the pen.

Having described these pens, I must point out that the less time you spend riding within fences, the better your colt will perform eventually. Horses become dependent on fences, and if you ride a horse within the confines of a fence for years, he will still be a green horse. For this reason, I recommend spending as little time as possible in the pens when you start a colt. Spend only as much time as you feel is necessary to gain sufficient control so that you will be safe riding him in a wide open area.

In fact, if you are an experienced rider who has started many colts before and you possess a solid independent seat, using this partnership-building method of starting colts will enable you to do it all without using a pen. You can build a relationship with your colts that will let you get on, beginning with the first ride, without any concern for runaway or lack of control. All you would need in this case is a fence with a solid post in order to apply the desensitizing stage of the program.

There are, however, two exceptions to the previous statement: if you work with a colt that has never been haltered, or if you make the decision to drive your colts. In either case you will need the large round pen. If you are starting a colt that has never been haltered before, he is likely to be skittish and looking to get away from you. You will need the confinement of the round pen to gain his trust. If you are going to drive your colt, it is necessary to begin inside a round pen for reasons of safety and control.

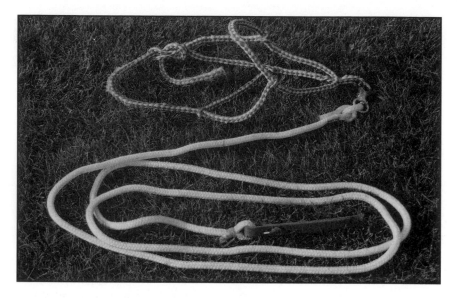

A rope halter that features no metal parts, as well as a 12-foot-long lead rope are the basic tools you will use to define much of your colt's foundation for optimum performance.

HALTER AND LEAD ROPE

Since most readers and horse owners do not own a round pen, this book will show you how to develop a round pen in your horse's mind without having to build one. Your halter and lead rope will set the boundaries of an invisible round pen. For this reason they deserve special attention.

The halter you use to start your colt should be made of synthetic rope. This is important, as a rope halter has no metal parts to it. Because it is softer than a nylon webbing halter, it bends better along the lines of the colt's head and gives immediately as the colt gives to the pressure on his head.

Wrap padding around the nosepiece of the halter to prevent chafing until the colt learns to bend and give to the pressure. Once the colt has learned to soften his body and bend as he feels the slight pressure of the halter on the side of his head, you may remove the wrapping.

While the halter is one important component of your invisible round pen, the lead rope is the other. Your lead rope should be a minimum of 12 feet in length to allow for tying your colt long at the fence during the desensitization process. The long lead rope also permits more control of your colt as you allow him to make his own decisions about bolting away or staying with you during the entire ground training process.

The lead rope may be made of braided cotton or nylon. My personal favorite is made of one-half inch anchor line, such as that used for sailboats. The material is soft, does not unravel as you twirl it, and as lead ropes go, is fairly inexpensive. I tie a popper made of leather at one end of the rope to give it weight. The weight makes it easier to twirl and drive the colt. I use a half-hitch and stitching to tie a large snap at the other end.

This halter and lead rope are the means by which you will teach your colt to bend and give to pressure. They are the tools you will use to define a specific area around you out of which they may not exit: your invisible round pen.

FLAG

The flag is a fiberglass driving whip a minimum of 6 feet in length with a plastic bag attached to the end of it. It serves as an extension of your arm. It lets you work your colt from a distance until he is ready to accept the touch of your hand. It allows you to reach your colt and touch him in places where he may kick without putting you at risk. It lets you move your colt back and forth as if you were touching him on the hip. It serves to desensitize your colt and get him ready for saddling without having to hobble him. It encourages the colt to bend and move his body in a relaxed fashion when he feels either mental or physical pressure.

The flag is not to be used as a whip to flog the colt when you get frustrated with his progress. It is not to make him go forward when he does not want to lead. These are misconceptions that greatly reduce the long-term effectiveness of this and any other approach to starting a colt. Be sure you follow the steps outlined later in the book so that you avoid misusing the flag.

SADDLE

Your colt-starting saddle must be of good quality. Since at times it will be necessary to saddle the colt with one hand while holding onto him with the other, your saddle should be sufficiently light to manage this. If you start a lot of colts, it may be worthwhile to purchase a saddle specifically for starting colts. Otherwise, the saddle you currently own will do.

A critical part of a saddle is that it fits you and the colt correctly. Large saddles usually do not fit colts since they are young and often small with still under-developed withers. It is unsafe to mount a colt saddled with a saddle that slides over his withers or rocks from side to side because it is too wide or too narrow at the gullet.

Do not be concerned about the shape of the seat of your saddle, or the swells and cantle being specifically designed to ride colts and help you ride a spooked, bucking colt. The method I discuss in this book should let you on colts without ever experiencing such activity. If the colt is going to buck, you should read the signs and avoid mounting.

Equip your saddle with safe latigos and cinches. As you saddle up a colt for the first time, you do not want to have a latigo break and a saddle roll under the colt's belly. Nor is it the time, as you place the saddle on the colt, to look for the hole punch and add a notch so the cinch will fit. Assure yourself of the good condition and adjustability of every aspect of the cinches, including the state of the cinch itself, before you approach the colt with the saddle.

I recommend using a neoprene cinch on the front of your colt-starting saddle. The neoprene is soft and extends under the cinch buckle, preventing the development of cinch sores on soft-skinned, often overweight colts.

Always use the back cinch when saddling a colt for the first few times, even if you will never need it afterwards. There are two reasons for this. First, a back cinch helps keep the saddle in place if a colt bucks. Second, someone someday may ride the colt with a back cinch–rigged saddle, and if the colt has never felt and accepted the back cinch, a wreck may occur.

BRIDLE AND BIT

The bridle must be in good working condition. All attachments, preferably of leather, must be solid and safe. I do not recommend bridles equipped with Chicago screws for everyday work. The screws often work loose, presenting a danger to the colt and rider if the bridle were to fall apart during a ride.

Since you are going to ride with a snaffle bit, it is critical that your bridle features a throatlatch and browband. One-earpiece bridles are not suitable for snaffle bits. When you make contact with a snaffle bit, the bit rides up in the horse's mouth, transferring slack up the cheek pieces of the headstall. The slack often loosens the headstall sufficiently so that it slips over the horse's ears and falls off his head. Not a good situation when you are riding a colt.

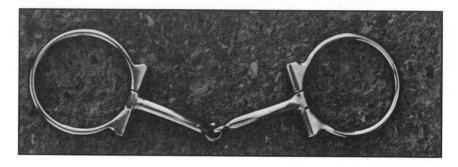

The Don Dodge Off-Set D-ring snaffle. This is the bit best suited to start-ing colts. Standard width is 5 inches. The straight sides of the off-set D-ring snaffle apply pressure on the side of the colt's mouth and make it easier for him to learn to give to the lateral pull of the hand.

The snaffle bit is the most effective bitting tool to start colts. Bosals, which are often used to prevent injury and pre-serve the colt's young mouth, are not necessary for this approach to starting colts. You see, injuring or otherwise over-using the colt's young mouth is not a concern in this case. The colt has learned to bend in response to halter pressure, and his body is able to respond to the bit pressure without resistance from day one. He is ready and able to respond to a snaffle from the moment it is placed in his mouth.

The best type of snaffle to use is the offset D-ring. Because of its flat cheek pieces, the offset D-ring offers more surface contact on the side of the colt's mouth. Therefore, when you apply pressure on the rein to teach the colt how to give to the bit, you activate the cheek piece and the mouthpiece. The mouthpiece puts pressure on the mouth while the cheek piece puts pressure on the side of the muzzle. These two pressure points make it more obvious to the colt and allow him to learn at a faster pace. The snaffle bit should always be equipped with a chin strap to prevent the mouthpiece from painfully sliding through the colt's mouth.

Avoid using bitting devices such as running martingales and draw reins when starting colts. These devices are certainly not necessary and are potentially harmful. Their use may build a dependency on the part of the colt or, worse yet, on your part.

3

DESENSITIZING

Desensitizing is the process by which a green horse becomes accustomed to the sight and feel of strange objects about him and on him. Depending on a horse's background and disposition, the desensitizing process may last as little as a few minutes or as long as several days. In any case, it is important to proceed slowly and gently since the essence of desensitizing is to gain the horse's confidence and trust.

While desensitizing can be accomplished in various ways, the approach described here serves two purposes: at the same time as it gets the horse accustomed to foreign objects around and about him, it also takes advantage of the horse's natural fear of strange objects to supple and strengthen him in preparation for performance under saddle.

The goal in desensitizing the horse is to let it be his idea to stand and accept the saddle and other foreign objects on and about him. This is accomplished by allowing the colt to move when an object frightens him. In allowing the colt to move rather than immobilizing him with hobbles, he learns that there is a place for him to go when something bothers him. Eventually, the colt feels in control of his environment and, as a result, comes to a stage of complete body relaxation. Rather than a violent reaction, the colt moves slowly about when something frightens him. Further body relaxation is attained by bending and suppling the colt as he spooks, hence combining desensitizing with responsiveness exercises necessary for good performance under saddle.

For this stage of starting your colt you will need a 6-foot-long whip with a white plastic bag tied to the end (the flag), a halter with a 10-foot-long halter shank, and a safe fence or wall to tie the colt to. The first stage in the process of desensitizing is called flagging.

FLAGGING

Tie the colt to the fence, withers height, with approximately 5 feet of loose shank. Stand at a safe distance behind the colt and wave the flag softly, or just enough to make the colt move. If a soft waving of the flag sends the colt thrashing about very hard, you are too close and are over-exposing him. Over-exposing means the horse is being exposed to a stimulus that is much too strong for what he is ready to accept. He is scared and feels he cannot protect himself in his current environment. Back away from the colt even further. The distance will let him think he can handle the threatening element, the flag, by simply moving slowly away from it.

Move back and forth with the colt to keep him moving to the left and to the right. Always move to the colt's hindquarters, never to his head. This is an important point to remember in order to prevent the colt from pulling back on the halter.

This colt is over-exposed as indicated by the high head and the tension applied to the lead rope. He has been scared to the point of jumping around and will not learn to relax, bend, and give to pressure in such a state of fear for his safety.

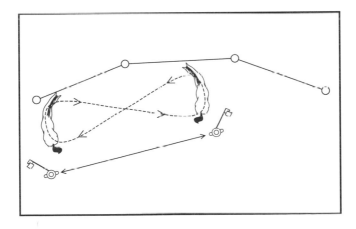

Flagging the colt will turn his natural fear of foreign objects into a tool for developing suppleness and strength. Move back and forth at a safe distance behind the colt's hindquarters, sending him at a walk or jog from left to right and vice-versa.

As you wave the flag and move back and forth, the colt will respond by moving away from the flag. As he moves away from the flag, he will bump the end of the lead shank and find himself having to give to the halter pressure on the side of his head and turn the other way. As he moves away from the flag, you also follow his hindquarters, and as he turns to face the other way, giving to the pressure of the halter, you wave the flag and send him on again. Back and forth you send him. As he goes to the left, he has to give to the halter pressure and bend to the right. As he goes to the right, he has to give to the halter pressure and bend to the left.

In the process, the colt learns to give to pressure on the side of his head. Soon, he does not put tension on the lead rope but rather has become so responsive to the light pressure of the tightening lead rope that he bends and turns before any tension is communicated to the rope.

As he turns in response to the flag and the halter pressure, the colt uses several muscles he normally does not use but will need later as he performs under saddle.

The hindquarters stretch and strengthen as he reaches deep under himself with his inside hind leg during the turn. The horse will use this strength and suppleness later in stops, rollbacks, lead departures, flying lead changes, turns around the barrels, etc.

The abdominal muscles strengthen as he rounds his back and lowers his croup for the tight turn away from the flag and the halter pressure. These muscles are necessary for stops, turns, and transitions.

The ribcage muscles on the outside of the turn stretch and supple and those on the inside of the turn contract and strengthen as he turns. The inside foreleg steps sideways as he begins to clear the fence with his head and neck in the turn, while the outside foreleg steps across in front of the inside foreleg. This lateral stepping of the forelimbs will be necessary in the turns. Suppleness and strength of the ribcage and the muscles that attach the shoulder blades to the ribcage are key to turns on the haunches, spins, turning in front of the cow, turning the barrels, etc.

Throughout the desensitizing process it is very important that you be attentive to the colt and reward any small change in behavior by removing pressure from him. To reward the small change in behavior, watch the colt very closely for signs that he may want to stop and look at you as you move him back and forth. As soon as you see the colt want to stop and look at you and the flag, stop the waving and take a step back. The colt will probably lick his lips as he stands there looking at you and the flag. This is an important change in the colt's behavior as he tries to deal with the threatening object. When this attempt on the part of the colt at dealing with his environment takes place, you must stop the stimulus immediately as a reward for the colt.

Keep flagging the colt back and forth until he stops and lets you touch him with the flag. As you flag the colt, notice the changes taking place in him: He will progress from a tense, very stiff way of moving back and forth, to trotting back and forth, to walking back and forth. When the colt gets to the stage when he walks back and forth, you will notice that he does not hit the lead rope anymore but rather bends in the neck and body, keeping the lead rope loose and stepping under himself with his inside hind leg. This is a sign that the colt is beginning to relax the muscles in his body and is learning to respond to stimuli by bending and moving rather than

The colt has been sent to the right and is now preparing to turn. Note the raised left hind leg, which is preparing to cross deep under the colt's belly. Also note the right front limb cocked and ready to step crossways in front of the left front.

The colt has completed the turn on a loose lead rope and is now walking to the left in a relaxed manner.

The colt has now traveled to the left as far as the loose lead rope will allow him. He is beginning a turn to the right. The right hind leg has stepped crosswise under the body, and the right front limb is stepping laterally to the right. His body is bent to accommodate the lead rope, which he has learned to keep loose.

The colt has stepped laterally with the left forelimb. He is now coming out of the right turn and beginning his walk to the right for the left turn.

by tightening up. Later during ground training, this bending of the body in response to the halter will be transferred to the bit in preparation for riding.

Advancing Desensitization:
The Round-Trip Around the Colt

When the colt shows signs of wanting to stop and licks his lips as you step back and let him stand still briefly, it is time to move on to the next stage of desensitization: the round-trip around the colt. The round-trip around the colt consists of rubbing the flag all around the colt's body, both from the left and from the right, without the colt tightening or moving any muscles. The colt is tied with 5 or 6 feet of lead rope, giving him plenty of opportunity to flee as the flag is rubbed on him. Because of this opportunity, it becomes the colt's idea to stand there and accept the object. The comfort level that the colt attains with foreign objects as a result of this exercise is key to his standing still for saddling and mounting. Therefore, the round-trip around the colt is an important step in preparing him for saddling and mounting.

To begin work on this stage of the desensitization process, wait for the colt to show you he is ready. The sign comes when the colt stops, looks at you, and licks his lips as he stands still. At this point, slowly move toward him, and gently touch him with the flag in the area of the withers. Watch to see if any muscles are tensing as you approach him and touch him. Tensing of the muscles is a sign of fear, and the colt is simply telling you that he is not yet comfortable with foreign objects this close to him. If the colt begins to move as you touch him, wave the flag, and send him back and forth. If he tenses but remains still, very gently move the flag toward his rump.

40

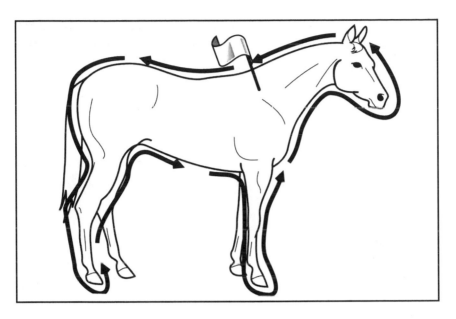

Begin the round-trip around the colt at the withers. Move toward the croup and continue down the back of the hind legs, all the way around the colt and back to the withers. Do not wave the flag under the colt's head or neck until he accepts the flag all over his hindquarters and back. Until the colt accepts the flag all over his hindquarters and back, he is much too unfamiliar with it. To wave it under his head or neck would cause him to pull back violently.

Keep moving the flag around his rump and down the back of the hind leg closest to you. Continue and move the flag up the front of the hind leg and spend some time at the flank, rubbing the sensitivity out of the area. If at any time the colt moves or kicks, step away from him, and wave the flag to send him back and forth again.

If you send the horse back and forth every time he moves or kicks, he will soon associate the wrong response, moving or kicking, with the less comfortable request of movement. By

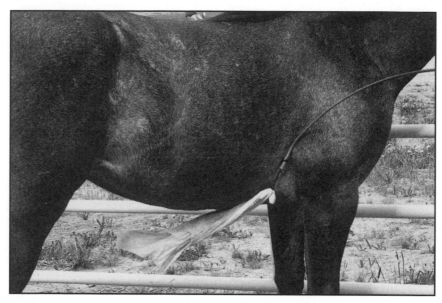

Be sure to rub the colt at the flank and behind the elbows at the cinch area. Also touch him on the lower part of the front legs since the cinch may touch him there when you put the saddle on him. Many colts are quite bothered if touched in this manner. Saddling difficulties become such because the trainer did not take the time to get the colt accustomed to being touched in the cinch area and on the front legs.

process of elimination, the horse will quickly learn that the desired response, standing still, is more comfortable than the wrong response. Again, standing still becomes the horse's idea, and he does it willingly.

Continue the process of the round-trip until you can go all the way around the horse from his withers, down to his rump, down the back of the hind leg, up the front of the hind leg, forward under the abdomen, down the back of the front leg, up the front of the front leg, forward under the neck, toward the nose under the jaw, up around the lips and nostrils, up the bridge of the nose, around the ears, and finally down the neck.

Continue the process working from the other side of the horse. Your goal is to be able to touch the colt all over his body with the flag without his tensing up at any time. Once you can touch the colt with the flag, shake the flag above his head and neck, as well as above his back where you will be sitting. This will further desensitize the horse and prepare him for the saddling session soon to come. It may take anywhere from 10 minutes to 2 or 3 hours of steady work to achieve this level of acceptance. You should not attempt to saddle the colt until you can do this round-trip.

Work on the desensitizing process until the colt moves back and forth along the fence in a relaxed and quiet manner, bends through the body as he turns, and steps deep under himself with his inside hind leg while he crosses his front legs to come out of the turn. Once he responds to the waving of the flag in this fashion, and stands still and relaxed for the round-trip from both sides, the colt is ready for the next step in the training process.

4

SUPPLENESS AND MOVING THE LIMBS

Suppleness along the fence and moving back and forth as a response to the flag is the beginning of preparation for maximum performance. Once the colt is comfortable and moving without resistance along the fence, he is ready for the advanced stage of suppleness development. This stage takes place away from the fence with the colt in hand (for those colts that are rather quiet). If your colt is the type that needed work from the back of a trained horse prior to the flag work along the fence, you may want to perform the first parts of this stage of suppling and training from a horseback. Here again, the same caution applies that did at the earlier stage of work from horseback.

The purpose of the exercise is to further the suppling and strengthening process begun along the fence by asking and expecting more bending of the body and displacement of the limbs. An important benefit is that the colt learns to direct his attention to you. He learns that what you do, where you go, and how you move affect what he is soon going to do. As a result, he begins to watch you rather than any interesting or even scary things he may find in the environment. Soon you have your colt's undivided attention, not because of fear but rather because of consistent, quiet insistence.

PROCEDURE

The method by which you will achieve this ultimate suppling is simple. With your colt haltered, stand next to his left shoulder, facing the rear. Hold the lead rope in your hand closest to the colt at approximately 3 to 4 feet away from the halter. Make sure your elbow and arm are next to your ribcage. This detail will become important when the colt resists the bending and movement of his limbs. If you are doing this exercise from horseback, resistance from the colt will easily be overcome by your saddle horse.

Holding your arm solid against your ribcage, walk toward the horse's right hip. This movement on such a short lead rope will cause the halter to put pressure on the horse's head. In response to the pressure, the colt will bend and move around you. As he moves, continue to walk toward his hip at a steady pace, encouraging him to move his limbs and bend his entire body.

At the beginning, the colt will resist the movement and appear to freeze his limbs rather than bend and move. At this point, his resistance causes a strong pressure on the lead rope. You feel this resistance in your hand and need to continue walking into his hip as he resists. If necessary, lean your upper body forward toward his hip to help increase pressure on the halter. As you increase the pressure on the halter, the colt will begin to move again by displacing one of his legs.

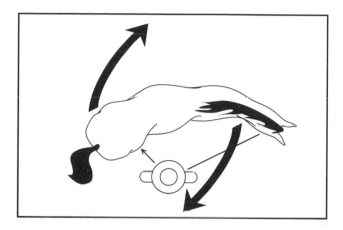

To lay a foundation for ultimate suppling, hold the lead rope short with your elbow close to your ribs. Face the rear of the colt, and walk toward his hip. In response to pressure from the halter on his head, the colt will bend and move around you. As he moves, continue to walk toward his hip until he steps laterally with all four limbs in a fluid, free manner from a light contact of the lead rope.

As the author walks toward this colt's right hip, the colt bends the body and steps laterally. Notice the left front limb preparing to lift and step sideways in front of the body.

Here the colt begins to step laterally with the right hind limb. Observe the large lateral step he is about to complete with the left front limb, crossing clear over the right front limb.

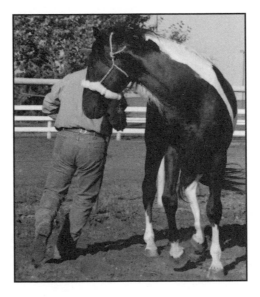

Again the colt is standing on two feet, preparing himself to step laterally to the right with the right front limb and to the left with the left hind limb.

The movement of the limbs in response to the pressure from the halter is key to the relaxation and suppleness we desire in the colt throughout his performance life. This movement is not possible unless the colt relaxes and gives to pressure. This relaxing in response to pressure, rather than the alternative bracing and fear, is the foundation of a relaxed colt during the first ride and the ultimate ability to use himself to his full potential.

As the colt supples up and develops the ability to move his feet, you will notice that he takes bigger steps than at the beginning. The lateral steps to the right taken by the front legs as you walk toward the colt's right hip prepare him well for the turnarounds we need later in western performance. The large muscles that attach the front limbs and shoulder blades to the ribcage must stretch and strengthen in order for the colt to find relief from the pressure of the halter. At the same time as the front limbs step laterally to the right, the hind limbs move laterally to the left. The right hind limb moves deep under the colt's body, stretching and suppling the large muscles on the outside of the colt's right hip and strengthening the muscles on the inside of the right limb. The left hind limb steps laterally and forward to the left, strengthening the muscles on the outside of the left hip and stretching the muscles on the inside of the left hind limb.

Walk toward the colt's right hip until you feel a small change in behavior. In this case, the small change in behavior is characterized by less resistance to the lead rope as you walk toward the colt's hip and take up the slack. When you feel this small change in behavior, stop and let the colt rest for a few minutes. This is a good time for bonding. Pat the colt between the eyes or rub him on the top part of his neck.

Now bent to the left, the colt is preparing to step deep under himself and to the right with the left hind limb.

Evidence of the degree of suppleness and strength developed by this exercise is shown by the large portion of the colt's torso to the right of his hip.

Move to the left side of the colt, and repeat the process until you feel a small change in behavior on this side. Reward the small change by resting the colt, and repeat on the right side. Continue to work each side of the colt until he offers no resistance to you as you walk toward his hip at a regular walking pace. At this stage, the colt is ready to yet further develop suppleness and strength as he experiences response and respect.

5

RESPONSE AND
RESPECT

Response and respect are paramount to safety, as well as extremely useful. While some colts respond to the halter but are not fearful of the handler, others shoulder into the handler when something frightens them. Yet, others are ready to bolt and run away from the handler at the smallest move or happening, while some are disrespectful, sluggish, and non-responsive.

The response and respect exercise gives the colt the opportunity to develop respect for the halter pressure around his head. In addition, it provides an opportunity for the colt to develop confidence in the handler as he learns that there is a safe and comfortable place for him to go to when something is threatening. That comfortable place is a small, invisible round pen next to the handler. In this small circle within arms' length of the handler, the colt learns that all scary objects are non-threatening. He learns that as long as he is in this small circle, he is more comfortable than if he tries to bolt and run away from the threatening object.

While he can move around the handler, the horse learns it is uncomfortable when he moves into the handler's personal space. Such respect for the handler's personal space is useful in any ground handling or basic handling situation.

In the process of practicing the response and respect exercise, the horse also learns to respond to the indications of the handler's arms and hands. As you stretch your arm out and show direction with the hand holding the lead rope, your horse learns to move in that direction. When you change hands on the rope and point the other way, your horse moves in that new direction. As a result, awareness of you as the handler, your body position, your personal space, and your body language develops into positive responses.

In addition to these mental benefits, the response and respect exercise further develops the horse's muscle structure. The suppleness and strength he began to develop along the fence in response to the flag is now associated with your body language. The deep engagement of the inside hind leg, the rounding of the back, the dropping of the tail closer to the ground, now take place as you tug on the halter to ask him to stop. The suppling and strengthening of the forehand muscles and the preparation for turning while under saddle take place as you twirl and ask for a change of direction.

Through bumping on the halter shank, twirling, and respect for personal space, the colt learns that relaxation and bending through the body are necessary to be comfortable in the small circle.

The result of practicing the response and respect exercise is a colt better prepared for trailer loading, saddling, bridling, bitting, mounting, turning, stopping, backing up, etc. Unless the colt is comfortable with the handler at his side and understands that he cannot run over the handler or run away from her, he cannot be saddled safely. Unless he is relaxed, he cannot bend to pressure—and bending to pressure is key to learning to respond to the bit. Unless he is relaxed and confident, he is bracing against the aids. It is impossible for the colt to respond correctly with the proper muscles while turning or stopping, or executing any other maneuver, when he is bracing.

DEVELOPING RESPONSE AND RESPECT

Once the horse bends readily on both sides as he moves back and forth along the fence and accepts the round-trip around his body, he is ready for the response and respect exercise. The exercise consists of sending or driving the horse around you at a walk or trot. While he walks around you, the colt bends in the body and neck, keeping the 3- to 4-foot lead rope loose. As you ask the horse to change direction, he should cross his front legs and pivot on his inside hind leg, driving forward from the hindquarters as he walks or trots the other way.

To practice the response and respect exercise, you will use the same 10-foot lead rope with a popper at the end and the rope halter that you used while working with the flag on the fence.

Untie the colt from the fence and bring him to the middle of the pen. Hold the lead rope approximately 3 feet away from the halter.

Indicate to the colt the direction you want him to go by extending one arm to the side while you twirl the tail end of the lead rope with your other hand. For instance, let's say you want the colt to go left. Extend your left arm and hand to your

During the response and respect exercise, the colt walks or jogs in a small (10 to 12 feet in diameter) circle around you, keeping the lead rope loose. In order to keep the lead rope loose, the colt must bend his body. The effort required to bend the body stretches the torso, back, hindquarters, and abdominal muscles on the outside of the circle while it strengthens the muscles on the inside of the circle. See how the colt crosses his front limbs as he walks the small circle.

left side and twirl the tail end of the rope with your right hand toward his right nostril.

As the colt begins to move left, immediately stop twirling the rope as a way of rewarding the small change in behavior—from a standing still position to a movement—however small the change was. The colt may move very rapidly and try to run away from the twirling rope, as if to say: "I'm outta here!" Or he may take one hesitant step and stop, as if to ask: "Is this what I was supposed to do?" In either case, it is important to stop twirling as the horse begins to move.

Twirling the lead rope with the right hand, the handler sends the colt to the left. The left hand tugs on the lead rope, putting pressure on the halter as the colt responds with an attempt at escaping the small circle.

If the colt bolts—which is not likely if you did your preparation work on the fence—simply tug on the lead rope just before he gets far enough away from you to tighten it up. The timing is important here. If you wait to tug on the lead rope until the horse pulls on it, the effect on the horse's head will simply be one of pulling, and he can pull much harder than you can. If you tug on the rope before he puts pressure on it, the halter will bump his head, and he will learn that it is not comfortable to "hit" the end of the lead rope. It is at this time that you set the boundaries of the invisible round pen around

61

you. Soon the colt learns that it is more comfortable to simply move ahead than it is to bolt. In fact, something unpleasant happens—a bump on the side of his head—when he gets further than approximately 4 feet away from you.

If the colt does not move as you twirl the rope toward his nostril and a distance away from him, twirl faster and closer to him. If he still does not move, let the rope tap him somewhere between his ears and his withers. If he still does not move, tap him harder and faster. Finally, if this is not sufficient, step out of the circle and walk directly and energetically toward his front quarters as you swing the rope. If the colt tries to back up rather than step forward, stay in your circle and put light pressure on the lead rope and the halter. At the same time, twirl the tail end of the rope toward his shoulder rather than his neck. The basic principle is simple: the more your colt resists the more you match the resistance. Remember, your role is to make the right thing more comfortable than the wrong thing.

As the colt learns to respect the twirling end of the lead rope, he learns that fear and discomfort with a situation is not a valid reason for running away. He can move, but he cannot run away. In fact, running away or bolting brings more discomfort than the situation or object he is trying to avoid. This lesson will be critical when it comes time to saddle up and mount the colt. But more importantly, a state of mind begins to take shape in the colt. He gets to the point where fearful objects bring about a measured move forward rather than a dramatic reaction.

If the colt takes a step and stops, begin twirling again until he takes another step. And so on. Your goal is to have the colt maintain consistent rhythm as he walks around you on a loose shank while bent in the body—not just the neck but the torso

Sending the colt to the right. The right hand holds the lead rope, and the right arm extends to give the colt direction. The left hand holds the tag end of the lead rope and twirls it in the air to drive the colt in the new direction. The colt steps crosswise with his front legs in order to turn, developing the ability to turn in a flat, smooth fashion.

as well. Your feet should not move unless absolutely necessary. The idea is to develop suppleness and response in the horse, not in you. Therefore, draw an imaginary line around your feet—1¹/₂ to 2 feet—and stay in this circle.

Be sure the colt keeps the lead shank loose as he walks around you or tries to escape. In the process of ensuring this loose shank, you will bump the halter every time he puts pressure on the lead rope, and the colt will learn to respond to pressure by bending in the body. This bend in the body is indicative of suppleness and strength being developed in the muscles of the moving parts of the colt's body. It is important to the bitting process, which takes place before you ride your horse, and it is essential preparation for optimum performance under saddle.

Once your colt walks around you in a somewhat consistent rhythm, it is time to stop him and have him change direction. To stop the horse, simply slide your right hand down the rope and put light pressure on it, causing your horse to face you as he stops. This is important because in order to face you as he stops, your horse needs to further bend in the body as he reaches under himself with his inside hind leg. This process supples and strengthens him even more in preparation for all the exercises you expect him to perform under saddle.

Now send the horse to the right by extending your right arm and twirling the tail end of the rope with your left arm. In order to respond to the twirling, your horse will need to move his shoulders sideways toward your right. This movement of the shoulders can only take place if your colt steps laterally with his front legs. Here is the other benefit of stopping and turning your colt during the response and respect exercise. Your colt is developing not only more awareness of your body language and more suppleness and strength in the midsection and hindquarters, but also more suppleness and strength in the forequarters as he comes out of the turn in response to the twirling. The lateral stepping and crossing over of the forelimbs that your colt executes here is exactly the same movement that will be required of him later while working cattle, spinning during a reining pattern, or changing direction on the rail in a western pleasure class.

Be careful with the timing of your twirling. As soon as the colt begins to move, stop twirling in order to reward the small change in behavior and confirm that this particular response

This colt comes out of a change of direction to the left. He has crossed his front limbs over and moved his shoulders. Still bent to the right as he comes out of the turn, within the next two or three steps he will move his shoulders away from the handler and bend left as he begins the walk on a small circle to the left.

was the desired one. Again, be sure he keeps the lead rope loose as he walks around you.

Have your colt walk to your right until he has attained some sort of rhythm, then stop and turn to the left again. Continue the response and respect exercise until the colt walks around you in both directions and in a consistent rhythm while maintaining a bend in the torso and a loose shank. When you change direction, your colt should be relaxed and consistent at stepping under himself with his inside hind leg and crossing over with his forelegs.

Once he has achieved this degree of proficiency, and responds to and respects your body language and your personal space, he is relaxed. Also he is much more desensitized and responds to unfamiliar objects by simply moving forward at a walk into a small area evidently defined by an invisible fence around you. As he moves into this small round pen around you, he is not hindered by fear, but rather his response to fearful objects has been conditioned to bending and relaxing instead of bracing and bolting. Your colt is ready for the saddle and the bridle.

RESPONSE AND RESPECT AND BASIC HANDLING

The safe use of a horse depends much on the quality and quantity of the basic handling he has received. Such things as catching, leading, tying patiently, and having its feet picked up are essential parts of the initial training process. A horse that does not tie patiently will not devote much attention to the rider when under saddle. A colt that won't have his feet picked up is dangerous to be around since he does not tolerate being touched on the lower legs.

The response and respect exercise prepares your colt for these necessary basic handling responses. After having worked along the fence and in a small circle around you, your colt is much more relaxed and will likely let you touch him on the lower legs. (If not, go back to the flag, and touch him until he accepts it in a relaxed manner.) Begin to lift his foot up and hold it up for a few seconds at a time. Continue to work with each foot, lifting and holding only as long as your horse is relaxed through the process. As soon as you feel and see tension in your horse, stop the lifting of the foot, and stay there for a few seconds until your horse relaxes. As he relaxes, let the foot down to the ground softly, and move your horse as many steps as necessary to further remove the tension in his body. As the tension leaves, start over.

Leading and tying is a natural result of the response and respect exercise on the fence. During the exercise, your horse learned to respond to the halter pressure on his head and, consequently, halter trained himself in the process.

Regardless of the amount of handling your horse had prior to the beginning of this chapter, if you have done everything correctly in the way of process and timing, by now you should be able to catch your horse, lead him to a designated area, tie him, and pick up all four feet. Your horse should be able to remain tied for a minimum of ten minutes and demonstrate that he can stand patiently.

6

SADDLING

Saddling is, of course, a necessary step in the training of the green horse. While it certainly is possible to school a horse without a saddle on him, willing acceptance of the saddle is fundamental to developing the young horse's full performance potential. However, saddling is often the time when problems begin to develop. A colt that is relaxed and trustworthy suddenly becomes skittish and bolts away at the sight of any foreign object. Many a young horse's fear of foreign objects is confirmed as he runs away from the handler with a saddle bouncing on his croup.

Saddling does not have to be a troublesome experience for the young horse. It does not have to be a dangerous stage in the starting process. If your colt has been desensitized, accepts the round-trip around him, moves his limbs in a relaxed and rhythmic fashion as you move around him, and responds with respect, there should be no problem placing the saddle on his back and doing up the cinches.

In this chapter, I will take you through the procedure for safe and effective saddling of the colt. I will show you how to use the saddle to further desensitize the colt. In addition, you will see how to further develop the suppleness and strength needed for maximum performance.

PROCEDURE

Hold the horse in hand with a loose shank. Remember, tying or hobbling the colt means he stands there because you force him to do so. You want him to stand there because it is his idea to stand there. If you simply hold a loose shank, he has the option to stand and accept the saddle or to run. If he stands, you have your first sign that he will likely let you place the saddle on his back.

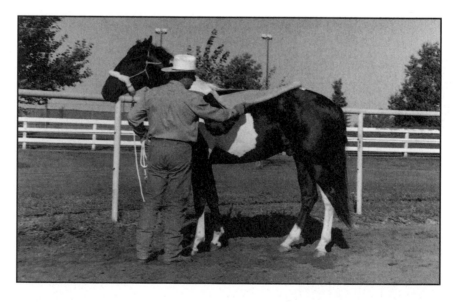

Hold the lead rope in one hand as you rub the folded saddle pad all over the colt's body. Allow the colt to move around as long as he remains within the small 10- to 12-foot circle you demarcate with the lead rope.

Use a saddle pad to begin the preparation for the saddle. Holding the lead shank in one hand, step up to the colt with a saddle pad folded in half. Rub the pad on his withers and then on his back, croup, neck, head, sides, and any other place the colt will let you touch him with the saddle pad. If the colt is really bothered by the saddle pad, so much that he tends to bolt and does not respect the small round pen you established during the response and respect exercise, tie him back to the fence and flag him some more. Otherwise, continue with the saddle pad until he stands and accepts it and stands still as you rub him with it from the left side as well as the right side. Rub the colt all over his body, including immediately behind the elbows. This area is particularly sensitive on some colts, and it is important to have them desensitized prior to saddling and cinching.

With the lead rope resting in the bend of your right arm, lift the saddle as you walk up slowly to the colt. Place the saddle on the colt very softly.

If your colt stands still while being rubbed all over with the saddle pad, it is time to saddle up. With the lead rope resting in the bend of your right arm, place the saddle pad on his back. Lift the saddle as you walk up to the right side of your colt. Place the saddle softly on his back. If the desensitization and the response and respect exercises were practiced correctly and sufficiently, the colt should accept the saddle without any bracing or movement. If he moves at all before you place the saddle on him or after it is on his back, a light tug on the halter shank should bring him into a small circle at the walk around you.

Any movement as you approach with the saddle or place it on him is a sign that more work is needed at this stage. Take the saddle off, and place it back on him again. Repeat this step as many times as necessary until the colt is comfortable with it and stands still while you place the saddle on his back. Once the colt stands still, let your cinches down, and walk to the left side of the horse.

With your lead shank in the bend of your left arm, stand next to your horse's left shoulder, facing his hindquarters. Run your right hand against his ribcage, and slowly but deliberately rub him behind the elbow in the area of the cinch. If he accepts the rubbing of your hand, continue to do so as you reach for the cinch.

Cinch the horse up slowly, progressively, and sufficiently tight so that you can move him around without the saddle falling off him. A tight, stiff body, hard croup and neck muscles, and a tail held tight between his hind legs are signs that he is not accepting the cinch pressure very well and may buck at any moment. Walk him around you as you did in the response and respect exercise, making sure that you stay clear of his way. Hard bucks are a sign that it was not his idea to

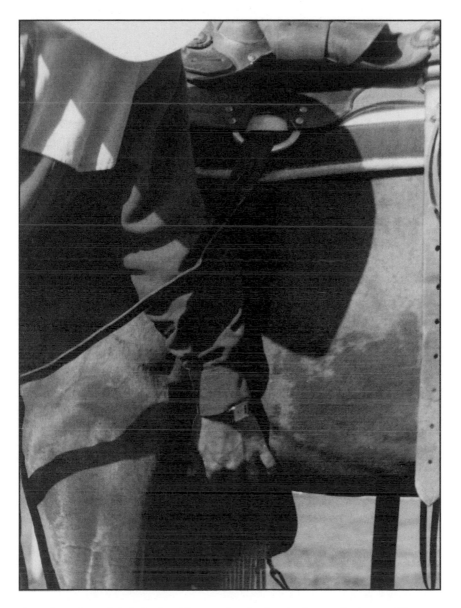

Stand at the colt's left shoulder, and rub the cinch area before pulling up and tightening the cinch.

carry a saddle and he was not ready for it. If he bucks too hard for you to control, let go of the rope and let him try to buck the saddle off. Once he stops bucking, remove the saddle, and rub him all over with the saddle pad. Repeat the steps of saddling, move the colt around you once he is saddled, unsaddle him, and start over until he moves at a walk around you without showing the signs that he is scared and may buck.

If the colt was properly desensitized and allowed to move around while you were saddling him, he will not buck at the cinch. Stop him and tighten the cinch some more, then move him around again. Repeat this step-by-step tightening of the cinch until it is tight enough to ride. Still standing at the horse's left shoulder, reach over and do up the back cinch.

This colt is uneasy about the feel of the cinch and saddle. As he crow-hops, the handler tugs on the lead rope, keeping him in the small, 10-foot circle delineated by the length of the lead rope.

Tighten the cinch slowly, breaking down the process of tightening into three or four parts, moving the horse at the walk between each part. Once the horse accepts the saddle on his back and the pressure of the cinch as he walks around you, take the saddle off. To unsaddle the colt, simply place the lead shank in the bend of your left arm as you undo the cinches. Walk around to the right side of the colt, and lift the saddle off his back. Saddle him again several times in the same session. This repetition of the saddling process several times the first day he is ever saddled will lead to complete familiarity and relaxation throughout the process later on.

Although already wearing a bridle, this colt still shows signs of fear as the handler flaps the stirrups along his sides. As he moves to get away from the noise and motion of the stirrups, the handler lets him move but keeps him in the small circle by tugging on the reins. Soon the colt will slow down and eventually will stand still as he accepts the noise and motion of the stirrups. Because he is not tied or hobbled, it will be the colt's idea to stand still and accept these things.

Allow the horse to move around you if he appears to be a bit uneasy about being saddled. Moving around you at the walk is the conditioned response you have instilled in his mind as a result of the previous stages of the starting process. It is the way he now responds to frightening objects. As he moves around, expect him to maintain a loose halter shank and a bend in his body. In doing so you reinforce the fact that, in uncertain situations, relaxing and bending is more comfortable than bracing and bolting. This state of mind you are imparting to your colt will serve him and you all throughout the performance years. From the time you put the first ride on him, your horse will be more relaxed and more ready to learn than another colt that has not learned to respond in this fashion.

Once your colt accepts the saddle without tension and fear, proceed with the desensitization.

DESENSITIZING WITH THE SADDLE

Once the colt accepts the saddle, it is important to continue the desensitizing process using the saddle. Thoroughly desensitizing the colt while using the saddle will ensure that the noise caused by the leather or the movement of the stirrups will not result in fear and resistance at the time of the first ride and subsequent rides.

Flip the stirrups around the side of the horse, bumping him on the sides and the shoulders. Flip the stirrups above the saddle and let them hit the saddle seat. Create noise by flapping the stirrup leathers. Make large gestures with your arms as you move the stirrups up and down on each side of him.

Throughout this desensitizing process, if the colt moves around you, let him. Remember, it must be by choice that he

Once the horse has been desensitized with the stirrups, teach him to give to the halter rope and bend as demonstrated in these photographs: (1) Face the colt's hindquarters. (2) Place the lead rope on your hip closest to the colt. (3) Hold the lead rope with your hand farthest away from the colt. (4) Place your other hand on the far side of the cantle, and stay close to the colt's side as he walks around and struggles against the pressure from the halter. Eventually the colt will give to the pressure and stop walking, at which point you repeat the exercise on the other side.

stands there and accepts the noise and movement. If you keep him from moving, accepting the noise is not his idea but rather yours.

As he moves around you, the colt should be walking bent in the body and very attentive to the halter, not dragging you around or even hitting the end of the halter rope. When you give a slight tug on that halter rope, he should respond by bending in the body and keeping the lead rope loose.

If the colt is fine and relaxed with the saddle but begins to run around you when you begin the process of desensitizing with the stirrups, simply tug on the halter shank as you flap the stirrups and make noise and gestures. In doing so, you are taking advantage of the colt's natural fears of the noise and gestures to instill more suppleness, strength, and response. This is part of reinforcing the "relax and bend rather than brace and bolt" conditioned response to frightening situations. Be sure to keep the noise and gestures to levels at which you can manage control of the colt. Too much noise and gesturing puts you at the risk of over-exposing the colt to a point where he will escape your control and nothing is gained. Begin slowly and gently, and gradually increase the intensity of the moves until he stands still for all sorts of noise and gestures.

Repeat this saddling/desensitizing/unsaddling process several times during the first few days of saddling.

7

BITTING

Bitting is a very important step in the training of the horse. Since the bit is such a key element of your communication with the horse, it is important to lay a solid foundation.

We began laying a foundation for the bit when we first put a halter on the colt. At that moment, the colt wrote a behavioral script for himself based on the messages we sent him. Those messages dictate how he will accept the bit. If the messages were unclear, if the pressure relief came too late or did not come at all, if, throughout the desensitizing, suppling, and saddling process, the right thing was not made more comfortable than the wrong thing, the colt will have difficulty responding to the bit pressure in the desired way.

That is because throughout these processes, you are working with the colt's muscles, but first and foremost you are working with his mind. Throughout these processes you are developing a response pattern in preparation for the first bitting and all the following schooling sessions when the colt is guided by some form of mouthpiece. This response pattern

83

will dictate how readily the colt will progress in the development of bitting responses and how much of his performance potential he will allow the trainer to help him develop.

Evidence of the wrong response patterns is everywhere. Horse shows, rodeos, trail rides, local riding arenas, fun days, all feature plenty of horses with the wrong response patterns. These horses toss their head up every time the rider picks up on the reins. Or they open their mouth wide when pressure is applied for a stop. Many of these horses have very poor, if any, backup. Others will not turn to the left or the right, while yet others bury their noses between their knees every time the rider picks up on the reins.

Response to the bit is soft when the horse's mind is at peace and his body is supple. Time spent on suppling and relaxing the colt prior to the first bitting will make developing the correct response to the bit very easy and natural. Since the colt's muscles are supple and he can bend to the halter pressure, bending to bit pressure is also possible. With the ability to bend already in place, the colt simply has to seek the most comfortable way to hold himself when he feels pressure on his mouth. With his muscles able to respond as he seeks this more comfortable position, the desired response to bit pressure comes easily.

Difficulties arise when the colt, seeking a more comfortable position, is limited in his choices by the fact that his muscle mass has not been given a chance to acquire the suppleness necessary for him to find the comfort zone, specifically a bent body. At this point, more pressure has to be applied to the colt's mouth, as well as his mind, in order to bring about a response in the face of all that natural stiffness.

Based on these principles, it is clear that the better prepared the colt is for the bit, the less time it will take to bring about the correct response. Consequently, a simpler method of introducing the bit can be used and fewer, if any, difficulties can be expected in the process of developing the desired response.

In this chapter, I will introduce you to a simple and easy method for bitting colts. The method, which I term the relaxation method, is by far the most effective approach to bitting. Its success depends upon the thoroughness with which you have performed the previous steps in starting your colt. If he is ready, your colt will respond to light bit pressure with a minimum of fuss. You will not need to tie the bit up in his mouth, use an ineffective rubber mouth piece, and tie his head to the saddle. You will be able to dispense with hanging the bit in your colt's mouth for a few hours "until he gets used to it." You will be able to feel your colt's mouth and reward him for minute attempts at giving to pressure. You will further his suppleness, strength, and relaxation as you introduce him to the desired response to the lightest of all bit pressure.

Although not necessary if you practice the relaxation method correctly, driving with long lines is sometimes used with very skittish colts. For this reason, I will also discuss driving as a method of bitting colts. I will explain the advantages offered by both, and although one is not exclusive of the other, I will offer suggestions for making a decision as to which method you may wish to use. But first, let's discuss putting the bridle on the colt for the first time.

BRIDLING PROCEDURE

A colt will accept the bridle around and on his head if he can relate it to another familiar and nonthreatening touch around and about his head and ears. For this interpretation to take place, however, you must have prepared him for the bridle by touching him all over his head plenty of times without trying to put a bridle on him.

Be sure the colt can be touched all over the face, ears, and mouth. If your colt does not let you touch him about the head, you need to spend some time getting him comfortable with the process. Simply rub your hand over a part of his head that he lets you touch. Once he is completely relaxed, gradually move your hand to a part he is skittish about letting you touch. Keeping your hand on his head, return your hand to the comfortable part as soon as you see signs that he may move away from your touch. It is important to ease your way to the parts he is uncomfortable with and return your hand to a part he is comfortable with you touching before he moves his head away. Soon he will accept the fact that your aim is not to hurt him, and you will be able to touch his head all over. At this time, the touch of the bridle along the side of his head and ears is simply another touch that he no longer finds threatening.

Leave the halter on the colt for the first few times you bridle him. This is simply a safety measure. Should he get fearful and walk away, you can control him by taking the lead shank and bringing him back to you.

Move slowly around the colt's head. Rub him all over with your free hand and then with the hand holding the bridle before you place the bridle in a position for bridling. Once your colt is relaxed and accepts the touch of the bridle all over his head and ears, he is ready for the bridling.

Stand on the left side of the colt.

Bring your right arm under his chin, and place your right hand over the bridge of his nose. This position of your hand cradling his head will help show him that there is no reason to

Hold the bridle with your right hand above the bridge of the colt's nose for the first few bridlings. The position of your right hand gives you control over the colt's head and facilitates bridling.

move his head away from the bit as you bring it up to his mouth. Many colts have been made hard to bridle because the trainer did not give herself the means to show the colt he had nothing to fear. Although the colt was well prepared for the bridle, he was given the freedom to move his head away, and there never was an indication that this was not the desired response.

With your right hand rubbing the bridge of the colt's nose, bring the bridle up the front of the colt's head with your left hand.

Hold the cheek pieces of the bridle with your right hand as you rub the colt.

Lower your left hand, and with your fingers separate the chin strap from the mouthpiece.

Press your left thumb against the lower jaw of your colt's mouth, in the area of the inter-dental space. Rub back and forth in small circular motions until your colt opens his mouth.

As the colt opens his mouth, gently lift your right hand and the bridle while you guide the mouthpiece of the snaffle bit into his mouth. The colt will chew the bit and move the mouthpiece with his tongue. This is a completely natural reaction and will go away as soon as he learns the desired responses to bit pressure.

Hold the top of the bridle with your right hand while you press at the base of the left ear and slide the bridle over it. Follow with the right ear.

If your colt was ready for the bridle and you did everything right, this process should have taken place without a fuss. If he tossed his head and tried to escape, he was not quite ready or your coordination was not up to par. In either case, remove the bridle, being very careful not to bump him with the bit, and bridle him up again several times.

Adjust the bit as you would for an older horse, so that the mouthpiece touches the corners of the lips. Do not worry if the horse puts his tongue over the bit, with time he will learn to "carry" the bit in his mouth, keeping his tongue under the mouthpiece. If you choose the relaxation method to teach your colt to respond to the bit pressure, he is now ready to begin.

THE RELAXATION METHOD

The relaxation method is the most effective way of introducing a colt to the desired response to bit pressure. In fact, it is so effective that the training program is advanced by several days or even weeks and perhaps months by using this method. The reason it is so effective is best described by its name: relaxation. This method enables the colt to learn the desired responses without experiencing the fear, pain, and evasions that other methods of bitting cause. Regardless of what other method you may choose, none will provide you with the same opportunity to feel your colt's mouth during this critical development stage. None of the other methods will bring about such profound suppleness and strength in the muscular structure. No other bitting method will let you connect so closely with your horse's mind.

To apply the relaxation method while bitting your colt, simply repeat the same exercises you performed with the halter in Chapter 4. Stand at the colt's left shoulder, facing his hindquarters. Hold the left rein in your left hand with your elbow bent at a ninety-degree angle and held close to your body. Holding your arm solid against your ribcage, walk

Another way to apply the relaxation method of bitting the colt is as follows. Stand on the left side of the colt facing the rear. Run the left rein above your left hip and hold it in your right hand. Stretch your left arm above the seat of the saddle and hold the far side of the cantle with your left hand. Walk toward the rear of the colt as you use voice commands to encourage him to move. The pressure the bit puts on his mouth will cause him to bend in search of the most comfortable position. Keep moving as he moves, applying pressure on the bit with your hip if he stops.

toward the horse's left hip. Holding the rein this way will cause the bit to put pressure on the colt's mouth. In response to the pressure, the colt will bend and move around you. As he moves, continue to walk toward his hip at a steady pace, inciting him to move his limbs and bend his entire body.

At the beginning, the colt may resist pressure from the bit on his mouth and remain very straight rather than bend and move. When you feel this resistance in your hand, lean your upper body forward to increase the pressure on his mouth as you continue to walk into his hip. In other words, when the colt pushes against you, push back until he gives. As you increase the pressure on the bit, your colt will bend and move his limbs. At that moment, the pressure automatically lightens on his mouth and he begins to associate response and comfort. He learns that the right thing is more comfortable than the wrong thing. Bending to bit pressure, moving his limbs, rounding his back, lowering his croup, and crossing over in the front quarters become his idea.

The movement of the limbs as a response to the bit pressure is key. It is this relaxation to pressure, rather than the bracing and fear, that forms the foundation of a relaxed colt. Relaxation, which is of paramount importance during the first ride, ultimately opens the door for the colt to use himself to his full potential.

As the colt learns to give to bit pressure, he will take bigger and bigger steps. The new and so far unusual movements of large muscle groups he learned to execute as we worked on suppleness with the halter, he now learns to associate with the bit pressure on his mouth. At the same time as the front limbs step laterally to the left, the hind limbs move laterally to the right. The left hind limb moves deep under the colt's body, stretching and suppling the large muscles on the outside of the colt's left hip and strengthening the muscles on the inside of the left limb. The right hind limb steps laterally and forward to the right, strengthening the muscles on the outside of the right hip and stretching the muscles on the inside of the right hind limb.

Walk toward the colt's left hip until you feel a small change in behavior. In this case, the small change in behavior is characterized by less resistance to the bit pressure as you walk toward the colt's hip and take the slack. When you feel this small change in behavior, stop and let the colt rest for a few minutes. Pat the colt between the eyes or rub him on the top part of his neck. Rub him on the croup, legs, flank, and any other place you may feel will further relax him.

Move to the right side of the colt, and repeat the process until you feel a small change in behavior on this side. Reward the small change by resting the colt, and repeat on the left side. Continue to work each side of the colt until he offers no resistance as you walk toward his hip at a regular walking pace. At this stage, the colt is ready to yet further develop suppleness and strength as he experiences bit pressure on the side of his mouth.

Once the horse has learned to give to the bit through this method, proceed to the next step. Again, this exercise is a repetition of the "response and respect exercise" described earlier with the halter, except this time the horse learns to bend and give to lateral pressure on his mouth.

Holding the inside rein shorter than the outside rein, move him in small walking circles around you.

After he has walked around you once or twice, lift the hand that holds the inside rein, and make contact with the horse's mouth through the inside rein. The horse should bend in the neck and body, stop his front feet, and swing his

Response and respect with the bridle reins. This colt keeps his body bent to the light contact of a loose rein as he walks the small circle around the trainer.

hindquarters around by crossing his inside hind leg under his belly. At this point, he will be facing you and standing still.

Shorten the other rein, and repeat the exercise in the other direction.

As you perform the exercise, you will find that the horse gets lighter and more responsive to the contact of the bit on either side of his mouth.

At this point you need to make a decision: "Should I drive the colt or not?" If your colt is very supple and gives to very light pressure of the bit on his mouth while performing the two exercises above, you may choose to proceed to schooling on leg aids and disregard the remainder of this chapter. Otherwise, read on, and apply the driving method of bitting.

DRIVING

Driving can be considered an alternate method of preparing the colt for response to the bridle bit. Or you can simply use it in conjunction with the relaxation method described above. While driving, you can establish a response to voice commands and prepare the colt for some degree of control in the turns and stops. Not all trainers include driving in their training programs. Many do not drive horses, while others drive only those horses that are perhaps a touch scared and need more familiarity with the basics before riding. Many of the horses you will work with will not require driving.

If you make the decision to drive your colt, you will need specific tools in order to drive effectively. A round pen is considered a necessity for driving. In the round pen the colt will tend to flow freely around you, making it natural for him to move forward and turn, the basic driving pattern. The round shape also prevents the colt from getting "stuck" in a corner and getting scared as you use firmer aids to move him on.

Equally necessary are a pair of driving lines. These may be specifically designed driving lines, or they may simply be lunge lines. Driving lines are generally longer than lunge lines, but it is possible to find lunge lines long enough to drive safely. Whether you use driving lines or lunge lines, they must be of cotton rather than nylon. Cotton is less likely to burn the horse as it rubs on his hind leg.

You will also need a piece of rope or leather strap to tie the stirrups together to keep them from bouncing up and down. Tying the stirrups also insures that your driving line is anchored to something solid when you need to apply pressure to turn or stop your colt.

Finally, a pair of gloves is a recommended precaution. At times, a colt may bolt and pull on the reins. In such instances,

94

gloves prevent your hands from sliding on the reins, and if your hands do slip, gloves will prevent blisters from the lines.

Once you have this equipment in place, you are ready to assess your colt's readiness for driving.

Before he can be driven safely, a colt must accept the touch of the stirrups on his sides, the touch of a saddle pad or other object on the lower hind legs, and of course, the saddle on his back. The colt must also be able to bend in response to bit pressure on one side of his mouth or the other. To drive the colt before he has attained this basic level of desensitization and responsiveness is risky. The touch of a driving line on the hock could send him bolting, and there would not be enough control of his mind and body through the bit to reassure him and bring him back to a relaxed and confident state. The mental damage caused here may take months to repair.

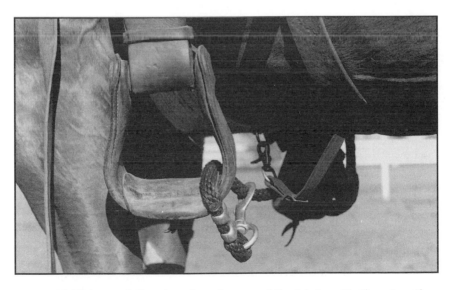

To avoid lifting and flapping the stirrups while driving, tie them together under the colt.

Once you are satisfied that these prerequisite responses are in place, it is time to take your colt to the round pen and saddle and bridle him. Once he is saddled and bridled, tie the stirrups together sufficiently tight to prevent them from flapping under the horse's belly as he moves.

With your colt standing quietly, uncoil the driving lines on the ground, one on each side of your colt. Step to the far side of the colt, and run one end of that driving line through the stirrup, and snap it to the cheek piece of the snaffle bit. Do the same on the other side. Now step to the end of the driving lines and pick them up, holding one in each hand.

Stand in the middle of the round pen. This is the safest position to be in if the colt bolts. It is also the position that affords you the most control. Were the colt to bolt, you could control him by tugging on the inside line. From your position in the middle of pen, you are in complete control. Maintain contact on the inside line, and wait until he slows down and stops.

Allow the colt to walk relaxed on loose reins before attempting to turn either way.

96

Standing in the middle of the pen, cluck or otherwise use your voice to get the colt moving forward. If he bolts, pull on the inside line gently until he slows down and settles. If he moves away slowly and hesitantly, give slack with both lines as you walk a small circle around the center point of the pen and in the direction of his hindquarters. Your goal is to have the colt walk in a relaxed fashion all the way around the pen several times and on loose reins. You will achieve this goal by allowing him to walk on loose reins, driving him forward gently with your voice when he slows down, and pulling on the reins to slow him down when he speeds up.

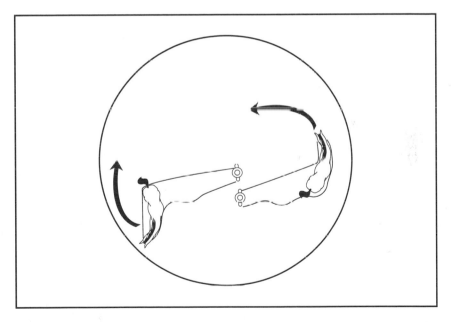

Stand in the middle of the pen for better control when driving. To turn the colt in the direction of the fence, simply tighten up on the outside line. To turn the colt toward the middle of the pen, or have him track on the inside rail, pull on the inside line.

Once your colt walks at a relaxed pace around the pen in the direction he started off, it is time to turn him into the fence and go in the other direction. Turning into the fence is critical at this time since the fence will help the colt associate turns with bit pressure on the outside of his mouth.

The colt completes a turn to the right toward the fence. In order to conclude the turn, he lifts the left front limb as he prepares to cross it laterally in front of the right front limb. The ability to cross over laterally has been developed by the moving of the limbs as well as the response and respect exercises.

To turn the colt into the fence and change direction, simply release the pressure on the inside driving line, and pull on the outside driving line until he is bent and positioned so that he has to complete the turn and move in the other direction.

Again, your goal in this direction is to have the colt walk in a consistent rhythm and a relaxed manner on loose lines. Once he does this, turn him toward the fence the other way, and walk again in the same direction you started with.

Here the colt concludes a turn to the left. His responsiveness to the pressure of the bit is evident by the lateral flexion to the left and the vertical flexion at the poll. The large crossover step taken by the right front limb is a further indication of suppleness in the front quarters.

Continue the routine, changing direction several times and working toward a more consistent rhythm and relaxation in the walk as well as in the turn.

Once the colt performs at this level, begin to ask for a smaller circle than that of the circumference of the round pen. In other words, if the round pen you are using is 60 feet in diameter, have the colt walk a circle of a diameter of, say, 40 feet. To do this, put intermittent pressure on the inside driving line. Work on a smaller circle until the colt has achieved rhythm and relaxation on the smaller circle and maintains a consistent size circle both to the left and to the right, on loose reins.

To stop the colt, simply say "Whoooooooa" and apply gradually increasing pressure on the driving lines.

Once your colt performs at this level and maintains rhythm and relaxation, you have gained a considerable amount of control over the speed at which he travels and the direction in which he travels. He is now ready for the next step in preparing him for mounting.

8

DEVELOPING
RESPONSE TO
LEG AIDS

A critical moment when sitting on a colt the first few rides is when we want him to move. It is often at this point that a colt will get tense and scared, and sometimes buck in an effort to free himself from what he sees as a dangerous environment. The reason for the tension and the fear, of course, is that the colt does not understand the leg aids applied. He has not associated the specific aids with a desired response, one that leads him to comfort. The reason is simple: It is very difficult to school the colt on the complete application of leg aids while on the ground. To school a colt on leg aids, one must be sitting on the colt. In this chapter, I will show you how to avoid creating confusion and fear in your colts by schooling them on a basic response to forward aids before you mount for the first time.

The basic aid we will use is simply touching the colt on the elbow or forearm with the side of the stirrup when we want him to move. We will add to the touch of the stirrup a voice aid such as a kissing sound or a cluck. Remember, the purpose of these leg aids at this time is to simply get the colt moving, hence the touching on the elbow or forearm rather than on the ribcage. The elbow or forearm of the colt is more sensitive; therefore, he is more likely to respond. In addition, it is clearer to the colt that he is to move his shoulders rather than elevate his back, something no colt is able to do at this time. After a few rides and as the colt begins to move, he will relax and eventually accept our leg aids. At this point, we will introduce and school on leg aids the same way we do with any other horse.

Walk by the colt's right side facing the same direction as the colt. Hold the reins in your right hand. Grasp the right stirrup with your left hand and touch the colt's right forearm or elbow. The colt should move forward at a walk as soon as he feels the touch of the stirrup on his elbow. Continue to school the colt on this exercise until you get several strides of relaxed walk as a response to one touch of the stirrup.

Once your colt is desensitized and accepts the saddle and stirrups touching him all over his sides, once he accepts the noise the stirrups make as you bang them on the saddle seat, and once he has successfully completed the bitting process, he is ready to learn a basic response to leg aids.

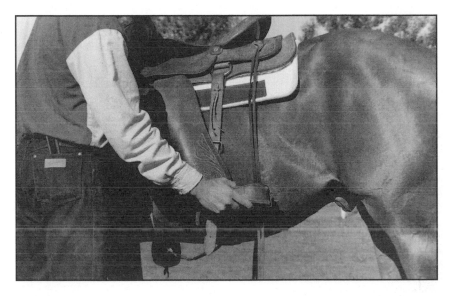

You may also teach the colt to move his hindquarters away from leg pressure by touching and bumping him with the stirrup behind the back cinch.

The procedure is simple. Stand by the colt's right side facing the same direction as the colt. Hold the reins in your right hand. Grasp the right stirrup with your left hand and touch the colt's right forearm or elbow. The colt should move forward at a walk as soon as he feels the touch of the stirrup on his elbow. Of course this will not happen since he does not know the desired response. At this point, tap the colt's elbow, beginning with light taps and gradually increasing the frequency and force of the tap each time until the colt moves. The colt will eventually move forward in a tentative fashion, taking one or two strides at the walk as if to say, "Is this what you want me to do?" When the colt moves, quit tapping immediately to show him that this was the desired response.

As you quit tapping, the colt will likely stop moving. Take this opportunity he gives you to reinforce the desired response by touching and tapping again until he moves. Repeat the process on the right side until the colt moves as soon as you touch him with the stirrup on the elbow or forearm. Then move to the other side of the colt, and follow the same procedure. The ultimate result is a colt that moves forward at the walk on loose reins for several strides without stopping. The desired response is instilled in his mind, which is a relaxed mind. When you sit on him, you can use this touch on the elbow to have him move gently and in a relaxed way—a nice alternative to the explosive response often associated with the colt that is not sure of the leg aids.

Now that your colt moves forward in a relaxed fashion when you touch him with your leg or stirrup rather than bucking out of fear, he is ready for the first ride.

9

MOUNTING

One of the most thrilling moments in horsemanship takes place when you put the first ride ever on a colt. It is thrilling because this may be the first of many great rides that will lead to an outstanding performer. It is thrilling because you have been looking forward to the first ride on a colt with all kinds of natural abilities. Or perhaps it is thrilling because this is the first time you ever put the first ride on a colt.

However, the first mount is equally one of the most dangerous moments in horsemanship. During the precious few seconds when the rider is in the process of getting on her horse, she is most vulnerable. Her seat has not yet made contact with the saddle, yet her feet are off the ground. Her base of support is very narrow: her foot in the stirrup. Were her horse to startle and move suddenly, she could find herself in a precarious situation. Sadly, many riders have been hurt and many horses have developed dangerous behaviors at mounting time. And regardless of how well schooled a horse is, what good is he if you are scared of the few seconds it takes to step in the stirrup and get on him?

In this chapter, I will detail a safe method of getting on your horse and list the warning signs you need to look for in your horse as you proceed to mount. But first, there are some things your horse needs to be able to perform before you should even consider stepping in the stirrup.

PRE-MOUNTING CHECK

A horse needs to be prepared for mounting just as he needs to be prepared before he can correctly perform any other maneuver, whether it be a half-pass or cutting a cow. Therefore, regardless of whether your horse is a young horse you are mounting for the first ride or an older horse with years of riding, give him the pre-ride test before you attempt to mount him. He should be able to answer the following questions and get them all right.

Hold the reins, and send the colt around you to the left and to the right. If he keeps the bend on a loose rein and walks in a relaxed rhythm, he gets high marks for this pre-mount check exercise.

1. If you hold the right rein and drive him forward in a small circle to the right around you, does he bend laterally and lower the poll as he walks, keeping the rein loose? If you can answer yes, repeat the exercise to the left. If the answer is no, your horse needs to learn to respond correctly to the bridle bit before you can ride him safely and effectively.

This colt stays completely calm as the trainer flaps the stirrup on the saddle and makes large gestures with his hands.

2. If you flap the left stirrup up and down and over the saddle as you stand to mount your horse, does he tense up and try to get away from you, or does he stand quietly, trusting that you are not about to endanger him in any way? If he stands quietly, proceed with the right side. If your horse says, "No, I will not stand here quietly while

With the lead rope attached to the snaffle bit on the right side, the handler steps away from the colt's opposite hip and gently applies pressure on the lead rope.

The colt bends and lowers his neck in order to give to the pressure on his mouth and moves his feet to find a more comfortable position: that of facing the trainer and with no pressure on his mouth.

112

you flap the stirrups!" you have work to do in gaining his confidence before you get on him. Your horse does not have to move in order to answer "no" to this question. Tension in the neck and croup muscles as well as the tail tucked tight against his hind legs are signs that he is not ready for the first mounting. Failure to prepare him fully by gaining his complete confidence will result in tension on his part and a potential attempt to escape an uncertain environment. Such an attempt is often disastrous to the rider and always disastrous to the horse's readiness to accept future training exercises.

3. As you stand facing the left side of your horse, attach a long lead rope to the cheek piece of the snaffle on the right side of your horse, run the lead rope down his side and above his right hock, and gently apply pressure to his mouth as you back away from him. Does he simply bend through the body and step around himself, keeping the lead rope loose as he turns to face you, or does he brace against the bit and try to escape the pressure by running and tossing his head? If he bends through the body and turns to face you, repeat the exercise on the left side. If he braces and tries to escape, your horse is not prepared to be mounted and ridden safely.

4. Touch the colt on the elbow or forearm with the side of the stirrup. Does he walk on calmly and with rhythm, or does he bolt? If your colt's answer to any of these four questions is incorrect, you do not have the elementary control necessary to be able to determine his movements and directions from atop his back. Spend more time preparing him for mounting by repeating the exercises detailed in the previous chapters.

113

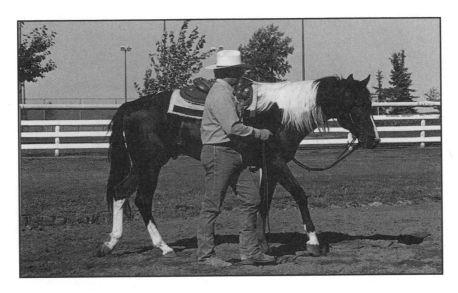

As he walks calmly at the touch of the stirrup on his elbow, the colt demonstrates his readiness to be mounted.

Once you are satisfied that your colt is prepared and can be mounted safely, proceed using the safest possible method. The method you select can vary, depending on your riding skills, the facilities at your disposal, and whether you have help available.

One method is to have someone hold on to the colt via a lunge line or lead rope as you get on. Another is to have an experienced rider on a snubbing horse hold the green colt by means of a lead rope dallied around the saddle horn. Both of these methods have served to start countless numbers of colts, however, they require experienced help and in the case of the latter, a quiet, broke saddle horse.

The method I use for mounting all colts is described in the next few paragraphs. It eliminates the need for an experienced

114

Patting the colt between the eyes is a trust-building element of ground training that will pay dividends, particularly when getting ready to mount the colt.

helper to hold the horse, as well as the need for a snubbing horse. The method assumes that you are an experienced rider and that your horse is properly prepared for mounting. I recommend mounting the colt in a small pen approximately 15 by 15 feet in size. This small enclosure prevents the colt from going anywhere and picking up speed getting there. If you have followed the instructions and have not taken shortcuts on the way to this stage of the process, there is no reason why your colt would want to go somewhere very fast. Nevertheless, there is no sense taking chances and giving him plenty of space to run if he were to get frightened.

HOW TO MOUNT

For this method:

1. Stand by the colt's left shoulder, facing the rear.

2. Holding the reins in your left hand on his withers, shorten the left rein to the point where your horse's nose is almost touching your back. In this body position, should your horse jump or spook, he would move in a circle around you, keeping you safe in the middle. Turning the horse's head away from you or letting him carry his head straight ahead of himself may result in his hindquarters bumping into you if he were to react negatively to the mounting procedure. Since your horse bends and gives to pressure, placing his nose in your back as you stand at his left shoulder should not be difficult.

   If your horse fights the bit at this moment, it is unsafe to mount him. At this point, watch for signs that your colt is not ready to be ridden:

   - If he fights the bend and tries to straighten his body rather than remain light on the rein

   - If he moves around rather than standing still

   - If he remains light on the rein but very tight and hard in his croup muscles

   - If he holds his tail very tight against his hind legs

   If any of the above items are true, he is not ready to accept your stepping into the stirrup. Move him to release the tension before going any further in the process. Once the signs of tension and fear are gone, continue on with step 3.

116

Stand by the colt's left shoulder, facing the rear.

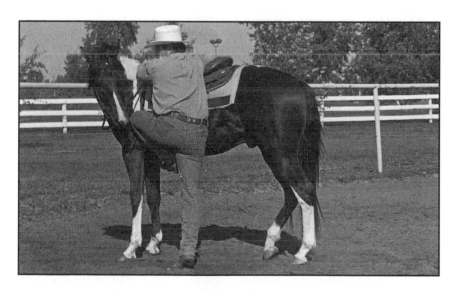

With your foot in the stirrup, ease yourself to a mounting position, being careful not to jab the colt in the ribs with your boot.

Notice the amount of bend in the colt's neck. The left rein is considerably shorter than the right rein, bending the colt's neck and thereby maintaining control as you step up in the stirrup. The right hand is on the horn, the left hand is on the mane.

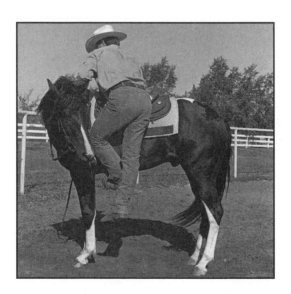

Ease yourself up the side of the colt until you feel or see signs of tension and fear. If the colt tenses up, immediately come down and move him around you. It is not critical that you stand all the way up into the stirrup the first time you try mounting.

3. Turn the stirrup leather with your right hand, and place your left foot in the stirrup no deeper than the ball of the foot. Avoid placing your left foot too deep in the stirrup. Should your horse spook, it may be difficult to step out of the stirrup and you face the danger of getting dragged.

4. Place your right hand on the saddle horn, and ease yourself up in the stirrup, leaning over your saddle as you get up. If your colt has been ridden but a few times or has never been ridden, do not attempt to sit on him at this time. Again watch for signs of tension and fear as you ease yourself up the side of the colt. Only ease yourself as high as the colt will let you without showing signs of fear. As the signs of fear appear, ease yourself back down, and move the colt forward to relax him. Then start step 4 over until you can ease yourself all the way up the left side of your colt.

5. Pat the horse on the neck, shoulder, and flank while you stand in the stirrup. Slowly dismount, and lead the horse forward a few strides or until he relaxes.

6. Repeat the process on the right side of the horse.

7. Repeat the process until the horse shows no signs of tension and fear. At this point, sit on the saddle softly. Continue to hold the left rein short if this is the side you mounted on. Keeping one rein shorter than the other gives the colt a measure of security and familiarity and gives you better control over his actions. Should he get scared and do something foolish, such as jumping ahead, you only need to bend your elbow to have control of his actions. Give the horse a few minutes to relax, then rub

If the colt accepts your climbing in the stirrup, stand all the way up, and stay there for a few seconds, then come down, walk him around you, and repeat the process.

Mount and dismount from the left and the right, patting the colt on the neck, shoulder, and flank of the opposite side while standing in the stirrup.

him on the neck next to the mane. Dismount, and repeat the process of mounting and dismounting several times the first day you do it.

Your safety while mounting green or unfamiliar horses depends on your ability to read the signs your horse sends you. If you are not familiar with the signs, spend some time with experienced trainers of young horses, and develop an eye for the tense horse and the relaxed horse. I repeat, when you denote tightening in the horse you are mounting, step down, walk the horse forward, and start over again. With repetition, your horse will accept the mounting process and become much safer all through the ride. Always be sure someone else is present when you prepare to mount a green horse or an unfamiliar or uncertain older horse.

IO

THE FIRST FIVE RIDES

The first rides on a colt are critical to the advancement of the training. They present you with the opportunity to confirm in the colt's mind the team relationship established during the ground training. They let you further softness and responsiveness. During these first few rides you can make large "relationship deposits" in your colt's mind, the kind of deposits that say: "We can work together. I am not going to harm you. Together we can have fun." In this chapter, I will discuss ways to make these deposits.

I have chosen to discuss the first five rides because for most colts there is a sort of natural progression after five or six rides. As you will see in the remainder of this chapter, there are clear objectives you will strive to achieve in the first four to six rides, after which you will adopt new challenges.

THE FIRST RIDE

Your goal during the first ride is to have the colt move forward in a relaxed manner at the walk to the left and to the right. It is not important to have the colt trot and lope on the first ride. Many colts have been scared and many have been set back in their confidence by riders who believed it was important to trot or lope the first ride. Whatever you do with your colt must foster this team relationship that you cultivated up to now. For the more than a thousand colts I have started, going faster than the walk on the first few rides would certainly have jeopardized this relationship.

If you reason that trotting and loping during the first few rides will save time, remember that training will progress at a faster pace if the colt's mind is at ease. Few colts' minds will stay at peace when they are asked to trot or lope during the first few rides. It is not that the colt has never trotted before. It is that the colt will not understand the aids necessary to push him into a trot or a lope. The result of the confusion is a need for strong aids that will scare the colt.

Assume that your colt lets you on his back without showing signs of fear and tension. Hold both reins in the same hand, with the rein on the side from which you mounted relatively short. To be safe and effective for the first ride, you should have to fully stretch your arm in order to release the pressure from the colt's mouth. Adjust the rein on the far side of the colt very long so as not to apply pressure on his mouth if you draw your arm back to bend him.

Shift your weight in the saddle from left to right very subtly and softly. This shifting of the saddle will brush his back and let him get familiar with the feel of your weight before you move him. If the colt tenses up, raises his back and his neck, and tucks his croup down as if to put his tail under himself, slow down the motion from left to right and let him relax. Start rocking gently again, and repeat the motion until he accepts it without showing signs of tension. Once he has accepted the left-right motion of the saddle, he is ready to move.

126

To move the colt, use the leg aids response that you taught him while on the ground. Still holding the left rein shorter than the right rein (or vice versa, depending on what side of the horse you mounted), tap the colt on the right elbow or forearm with the side of your stirrup. Use the same voice aids you used while ground training. As the colt moves a step, quit tapping. As soon as he stops moving, resume tapping.

During the first few minutes of moving the colt, you may want to keep a contact on his mouth with the inside rein. This is for security in case the colt tenses up and spooks. If your colt has been well prepared, he should not spook and take sudden action, such as jumping ahead or sideways. However, he is a colt, and there is always that possibility.

Let the colt move in the direction of the shorter rein for a few minutes or until he is moving in that direction relatively freely. At the beginning, the movement will likely be in a small circle since you are holding the rein quite short. However, as the colt lowers his head and begins to walk at a more consistent pace, stretch your arm, and let him walk on completely loose reins. While he walks on a loose rein, the colt will likely follow the fence of your small pen. At this time, you may want to get off the colt and mount again to reinforce the mounting/dismounting part of the program. However, if the colt was very quiet and accepting of the mounting/dismounting, you may simply lengthen this rein, shorten the opposite rein, and tap him with this stirrup to move him in a small circle in the opposite direction from which you were just turning.

Effect an opening rein to turn the colt toward the middle of the pen or toward the fence. It is the simplest of all rein effects and one the colt will respond to as a result of the ground training you have put him through.

Once your colt has walked freely to the left and to the right, you have achieved your objective for the first ride. Say

"Whooooa," and lift the slack out of the reins. Increase the pressure until he stops. As he does, release the pressure and shorten the left rein in preparation for a left dismount. The rein should be adjusted to the same length as when you mounted. Dismount in a smooth fashion. Put the colt away for the day. Your first ride should have lasted approximately ten to twenty minutes. It may have been broken up into two or three sessions of five to ten minutes, each joined together by mounting and dismounting practice.

THE SECOND TO FIFTH RIDES

The next day, begin the schooling session as you have done every day up to now: routine ground training steps followed by the pre-mount checklist, and practice mounting and dismounting. Once your colt again accepts every step of the way without showing signs of tension, sit in the saddle and repeat the steps accomplished while in the saddle yesterday. Hold your reins the same way as you did yesterday, and use your leg aids in the same fashion. Does your colt walk more relaxed than he did yesterday? He is able to take several steps without stopping, out of balance and rhythm? Do you feel more confident about stretching out your arm and letting him have a loose rein on the inside? Does he feel sufficiently relaxed, so that you are confident and able to ride with both hands on the reins? If the answer to all these questions is yes, he and you are probably ready to ask for the jog.

On loose reins, and keeping your shoulders behind your hips, tap him on the side of the elbow or forearm with the side of your stirrups. One stirrup at a time and alternating from left to right, tap him and use your voice aids until he speeds up the walk and eventually breaks into a trot, or jog, for one or two strides. Quit tapping as he breaks into the jog. This is the small change in behavior you are looking for. You must reward it immediately. Remember, ask for little, reward for less. You asked for the jog in a very quiet and polite manner; you will reward for the two or three strides you got.

Here is where a very common mistake is made that destroys many colts: As soon as the colt breaks gait into the walk, the rider pounces on him with both legs and whip or rein, and jumps him into the jog again. This scares the colt and often leads to bucking or running rather than the desired relaxed confidence that leads to greatness.

The colt will not hold the jog for more than few strides for two reasons:

1. He is not sure that it is the desired response. You have to show him that it is by removing the tapping of the stirrups.

2. He does not yet have the balance to carry on at the jog with a rider on his back. In this case, balance will come from doing more of it.

Therefore, after he has walked five or six strides and is relaxed again, resume tapping until he trots again. Little by little, two or three strides at a time, the colt will learn that continuous jogging is the desired response, and he will develop the balance to maintain the jog.

If you were able to achieve the jog on the second ride, you are doing well. If you were not successful at preparing the colt for the jog on the second ride, it is fine. Some colts will not be sufficiently relaxed to jog on the second ride, and pushing them to it will only scare them. If this is the case, be satisfied with the walk at perhaps a more consistent, slightly faster pace.

Other colts will not be able to jog in the small mounting pen because there is not enough space for them to go into a jog. You may have to ride them in the bigger pen if you are going to work on the jog, or trot. Are you prepared for that? Do you feel you have sufficient control to ride in the larger pen? If not, spend more time in the small pen, working and developing control at the walk. Once the colt is completely relaxed at the walk, turns to the inside and toward the fence as a response to the opening or leading rein, and maintains a consistent rhythm at the walk, move him to the larger pen. Repeat the same process of tapping on the elbow or forearm to get the colt into the jog. Again, ask for little, reward for less.

Continue to use the opening rein to get the colt to where you want to go. Turn him to the middle of the pen, and have him walk and jog on the inside rail. Then turn him toward the fence, and have him walk and jog out of the turn. By the third or fourth ride, when the colt is thoroughly relaxed at the walk, begin to introduce the outside rein and outside leg at the same time as the inside rein to guide the colt in the new direction.

The outside rein and outside leg build a wall that pushes the colt's shoulders in the desired direction of travel. This is the basis for neck-reining and guiding on circles and straight lines. It is critical that you begin applying these aids at this stage. Many colts learn to fall out with the outside shoulder at this stage because riders continue to use only the inside rein and lead the colt's nose in the direction of the turn rather than bringing the shoulders along with the head. As a result, these

Guide the colt through the turns by drawing the outside hand toward your belt buckle and opening your inside rein as you press your outside leg at the cinch. The result is a colt that responds correctly to the guiding aids by moving his shoulders right from the start.

colts are taught to shoulder-out on the turns. This bad habit affects every maneuver a horse will ever perform, from the transitions into the leads, to cutting cattle, to crooked stops, to poor turns around the barrels, to everything else. If your colt is to perform at his optimum potential, it is critical that you immediately prevent this bad habit from developing.

To prevent your colt from learning to fall out or shoulder-out in the turns and straight lines, you must change your turning aids paradigm. Rather than think of turning as leading the colt's head or nose in the new direction you wish to travel, you must think of it as pushing the colt's shoulders in the new direction with your outside rein.

To push the colt's shoulders in the new direction of travel, move your outside hand toward your belt buckle just in front of or immediately above the saddle horn. Of course the colt will not turn since this is a new concept to him. Reinforce the outside rein by applying pressure from your outside leg at the front cinch. Again, the colt is not likely to turn since all these aids are new. Effect an opening rein with your inside hand, and make contact on the corner of the colt's mouth with the inside rein. As you ask for a turn to the left, you now have pressure on the right side of the colt's neck and mouth, leg pressure at the front cinch on the right side of his body, and an opening rein applying pressure on the left side of his mouth.

If your colt is still walking forward in a straight line, and he probably is, increase the pressure on both sides of his mouth to rechannel some of the energy he is expending forward to a lateral direction. It is like water flowing down a stream. It travels in a straight line until it hits the bank, then it gets pushed into a new direction of travel. Your colt travels in a straight line until you form a bank or wall with your outside rein, outside leg, and inside rein, using the bit as a part of the wall. The pressure you apply with all three of these aids is determined by how much energy you need to redirect. If the colt turns at light pressure, that is all you need to apply. If he ignores light pressures, increase the amount from all three aids until you get the desired response.

Pressure from the hands on both sides of the mouth must be balanced so that the colt turns with a straight neck. There must not be bending of the neck while you turn the colt. If you allow the colt to bend his neck as he turns, you are allowing him to shoulder-out of the turn, a habit that is very damaging to performance. If the colt turns to the left but has his neck bent to the right as he moves his shoulders, increase left-hand pressure on the mouth and reduce right-hand pressure until the colt's neck is straight. The opposite applies if he turns to the left with his neck bent to the left. Decrease the pressure on the left side of the mouth and increase the pressure on the right side of the mouth until the neck is straight.

Keep the change of directions very minimal. A ninety-degree turn is absolutely unreasonable at this stage. Keep your turn to five or ten degrees. Small turns such as these are easily managed by the colt, and he is able to move his shoulders away from the outside wall. If you need to effect a pronounced turn, let the fence turn the colt. Better to let the fence turn the colt than to develop bad habits that will take months or perhaps years to correct. In two or three weeks of using your turning aids correctly, your colt should be able to make ninety-degree turns with no difficulty. And you avoided the common falling out or shouldering out problem. Congratulations! Your patience paid off.

To stop the colt during these first five or six rides, simply say "Whoooooa" slowly and lift the slack out of the reins slowly, giving the colt a chance to register that something is happening. If the colt does not stop as you say the word and lift the slack—and he probably will not—gradually increase the pressure on his mouth until he stops. Increase the pressure until he stops, even if it means much pressure on his mouth. As the colt stops, release the pressure and stand still for a few minutes, making the right thing more comfortable than the wrong thing. With a few repetitions, your colt will begin to stop without any contact on his mouth as you say the word "Whoooooa."

Work the colt in the larger pen at the walk and jog until he has achieved full relaxation and moves forward without breaking gait for several laps around the pen. Your goal while you work in the larger pen is to gain more control of the colt so you can safely work him in the open. As soon as you feel you can stop the colt, turn him in either direction, and jog or walk in a relaxed manner for several minutes at a time, it is time to move out of the pens for some informal schooling in an open field or larger riding area.

II

THE NEXT THIRTY RIDES

Every ride on a colt is critical to his entire performance career. This is certainly true for the next thirty rides. During this time the horse/man relationship is still fragile and can either be solidified or destroyed. The work that has been done so far in getting the colt to relax and bend can lead to maximum performance or problems that will never totally be eradicated. The handling and training over the next thirty rides will confirm in the colt's mind that the particular environment he is currently in is friendly and safe or that it is hostile and unreliable.

In order to achieve his full potential, your colt needs to experience exercises that will continue to develop his strength and suppleness. He needs exercises that will develop his ability to respond to basic applications of the aids, both mentally and physically. The exercises need to be done in a way that enhances the training program and does not limit your colt's potential. They need to show your colt the way to further training and eventually, perhaps, to a specialized area of performance.

In this chapter, we will examine the areas where you must focus your schooling time if you wish to further your horse's training. We will see how you can develop elementary shoulder control of your colt through bending. We will explore the way in which you can train your colt to guide in response to the neck rein. We will study the way in which you can have your colt back up in perfect frame and on very light contact. We will see how to establish a solid foundation for the stop— a foundation that will lead your colt to stopping deep under himself and even slide if the ground is suitable and he is shod for it. We will discuss how you can introduce your colt to turn-arounds and, as such, build a foundation of turning that will lead to the fastest spins your horse can deliver. And we will introduce your colt to the control of the hindquarters by talking about pivot-on-the-forehand and leg-yields.

First, we will discuss the benefits of schooling in an open field.

RIDING IN THE OPEN

An open field or large riding area is the best place to school your colt once you have the control and the confidence to ride out of the larger round pen. In confined areas, such as the round pen we have been using so far or the medium-sized riding areas (including 100 feet by 200 feet), a colt and even a well-trained older horse soon develop harmful habits. These habits are brought about by the fact that in such areas a horse is always forced to turn. Even on the long side of the area, a horse only travels a few strides in a straight line before he must prepare to turn the corner in which he will soon find himself.

The result of schooling in these areas all the time is a crooked horse, one with all sorts of body alignment difficulties. Some of these difficulties manifest themselves as falling in and falling out of turns and circles, the inability to travel in a straight line, or traveling in a straight line but with a crooked body. Other consequences of schooling within fences in small areas include difficulties picking up a lead or changing leads, backing up crooked, and stopping crooked.

In order to prevent these destructive habits from developing, a colt or mature horse should be schooled in an area no smaller than 200 feet wide by 450 feet long. With an area this size, a colt gets a chance to learn to travel straight and in a straight line before he gets to the corner and has to turn. Better yet is an area this size that is not fenced. Then you can ride your colt anywhere on the riding surface and ride off of it into a field anytime, enabling you to ride in straight lines for 200 or 300 yards before having to turn.

While riding in a field or pasture is great as far as riding straight lines is concerned, these places do not offer the right kind of footing for stopping and turning. Grass is often slippery even when dry, and it is certainly unsafe to ride on when wet, hence the idea of a large unfenced surface with prepared, groomed riding ground, set in the middle of a field where you can ride on and off the surface.

Riding in the open where the colt will have to cross creeks, travel down and up steep hills, maneuver around trees, and get used to birds and other forms of life is also very beneficial. These things will assist the colt in developing balance, and further the desensitizing process.

The most obvious advantage to riding in the open is the opportunity to blend schooling and simple riding. Working on

Riding in the tall grasses next to a lake gives these colts an opportunity to develop balance and accept such things as birds flying up unexpectedly, foxes, and other wildlife. As they deal with these elements, the colts learn to trust their riders for direction.

body control exercises such as shoulder-up or pivot-on-the-forehand and then riding the trail for ten or fifteen minutes before schooling again is a great way to get a lot of schooling done without the burnout and sour results associated with working in an arena all the time.

So, find a place where you can blend leisure riding in the open with schooling in wide, long areas. Your colt will develop to his maximum potential without the problems associated with small pens.

ELEMENTARY SHOULDER CONTROL

One of the most critical factors in achieving top performance is control of the horse's shoulders. Without control of the shoulders it becomes impossible for the rider to position the horse for optimum results in the maneuver he wishes to perform. For example, in the turn around the first barrel, your horse runs wide because his shoulders drift to the outside. Your pleasure horse's nose is out; his shoulder drops in toward the center of the pen. He picks up the wrong lead at times, and it is difficult for you to prevent it. Your cutting horse loses cattle to the left because you cannot position him to hold the cow on this side. At the last show, you picked up on the reins, and it cost you marks and money.

Wherever the shoulders go, that is where the colt is going. This is why controlling them is so important. The more control you have of your colt's shoulders, the easier it is to position him correctly for any maneuver and the more he will be able to perform. You will develop elementary shoulder control of your colt through the shoulder-up exercise. It is also called the small circle exercise.

The shoulder-up exercise is a forward movement during which the colt is bent in the direction of travel. As he performs the exercise to the right, his spine is bent to the right, from the poll down through the neck, the shoulders, and the torso, all the way to the croup. His head is to the inside of the circle. There is a definite bend in his ribcage as he contracts and shortens the right side and relaxes the left. The exercise supples and stretches the muscles of the neck, shoulders, torso, and hip. This suppleness and elasticity enables the colt to keep

141

his shoulders elevated while he turns either left or right. The result is more freedom during the turn and a better form at a greater speed.

What do I mean by shoulders elevated? Simple. A colt holds his shoulders elevated while he turns if he does not try to "cut" the circle or make the circle smaller than what you want. When you pick up on the inside rein and draw your hand to your hip, does your colt simply bend, or does he cut in and make a very small circle? If he bends and holds a circle of about 10 to 12 feet in diameter, he holds his shoulders up. If he feels as if he is turning very sharply when you pull on the rein but his shoulders fall when you ask for the turn, you do not have sufficient control of them to position your colt for optimum performance. You need to work on developing shoulder control.

There are two stages in the development of the shoulder-up exercise: elementary and advanced. In the elementary stage, you only concern yourself with the lateral bend. In the advanced stage, both of your hands and both of your legs are used as the horse executes the exercise. At the advanced stage, the horse flexes at the poll, lowers his neck, elevates his back toward the saddle, and lowers the croup as he reaches deeper under himself with his hind legs, particularly the inside hind leg. During the first thirty days of schooling, we only concern ourselves with the elementary stage of the exercise.

Your goal in the first thirty days of riding is to have the colt walk a circle 10 to 12 feet in diameter with consistent rhythm. As he walks that circle, the colt must maintain lateral bend on a loose rein without making the circle smaller. His topline should be level with his neck, about withers height. His chin should be about 20 to 24 inches from your stirrup, depending on the size of the colt. This amount of bend will challenge the

To perform a shoulder-up to the left, draw your left hand to your left hip, bringing the colt's head to the left. Be sure the outside rein is loose and passive. Apply leg pressure with both legs if the colt loses rhythm. The colt bends through the body as he steps deep under himself with the inside hind leg.

colt to hold his shoulders up. If you cannot bend your colt this much, or if he makes a circle smaller than 12 feet in diameter when he is bent this much, he is telling you that he cannot hold his shoulders elevated and balanced as he turns.

To bring your colt into a shoulder-up to the right, draw your right hand to your right hip and have the colt bend in response to the pressure on the right side of his mouth. Be sure your outside rein, in this case your left rein, is completely loose and passive, allowing your colt to bend as much as possible. It is important that you use only the inside rein at this stage of the exercise. If the colt has been properly prepared during the ground training aspect of this program, it should not be difficult to bend him.

If your colt tends to turn a very small circle rather than bending in the ribcage, he is dropping the shoulders. Release the rein, and ride him forward with both legs. As he takes a stride forward, your colt will rebalance himself and elevate his shoulders again. Were he not to elevate his shoulders, he would not be able to step forward. Take that opportunity to ask for the bend again by drawing your inside hand to your inside hip. As you alternate between riding forward with both legs and bending him with the inside rein, your colt learns to hold his shoulders up in anticipation of riding forward. Yet he also learns to move forward and bend in anticipation of the rein pressure asking for the bend. With time, he learns to move forward while holding his shoulders elevated all by himself. He carries himself in balance. He may need a few days and perhaps a few weeks to develop the ability to hold himself balanced, but he will get there if you alternate between the inside rein and riding forward with both legs.

It is very important that the aids be applied in an intermittent fashion. Place the colt's head at the right place, and give

A profile view of the shoulder-up exercise. The colt holds his neck level with his withers. He steps deep under himself with his inside hind leg and he steps laterally with his front legs, crossing the outside front limb in front of the inside front limb.

slack in the rein by lowering your hand toward his mouth. The stiff colt that drops the shoulders will immediately take his head away and straighten his body. Immediately, gently pick up on the rein, and bring his head to the inside again. It is the simple principle of reward and reprimand. If you hold the horse's head in the same position, he eventually will pull against you and will become dull in the mouth. He will depend on you for balance rather than learn to hold his shoulder up by himself. If you move his head and shoulders and then release the pressure, he will soon learn the benefits of responding to the aids. Once your colt bends readily in the ribcage on both sides and holds his bend on loose reins for several strides at a time without your having to correct him, you have achieved your goal of elementary shoulder control.

GUIDING

Guiding is the act of directing the colt's direction of travel. When a colt guides, he travels exactly where you want him to without pushing against one rein or the other. His body is straight from poll to tail, and he lets you determine within inches where he is going to place his front feet as he walks, trots, or lopes. The guiding colt responds to a very light, loose outside rein on the side of his neck.

School your colt on guiding by asking him to deviate slightly while walking or trotting straight lines across the pasture or riding area. Many riders begin to work on guiding from a circle. The circle demands pronounced turns that are too difficult for the colt to perform correctly. The very small degree of turn required to deviate slightly is easy for your colt to perform. Build on it all the way to sharp and fast turns, such as those necessary for a winning barrel run.

You have already been applying guiding aids in the large round pen and getting a hint of response. As you ride in the open, apply the same aids. Feel for your colt's shoulders subtly moving away from the wall of pressure created by your outside rein drawn to your belt buckle, your outside leg reinforcing the push, and your inside rein opened wide showing him direction. As soon as your colt responds by moving his shoulders away from the outside wall and changing direction ever so slightly, release the aids, and let him go straight for a few strides before asking again.

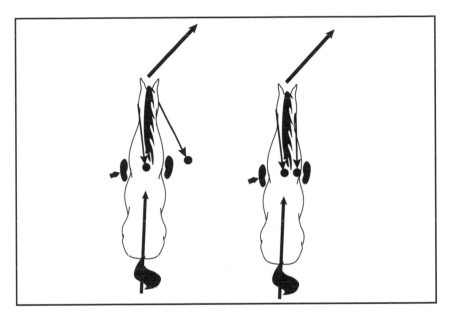

The aids for developing guiding. In the figure on the left, the rider pushes the colt's shoulders to the right by building a "wall" on the left side. To build the wall, draw your outside hand to your belt buckle, and apply pressure with the outside leg at the cinch. If the colt does not move his shoulders away from the rein, open the inside hand, and increase the pressure on the mouth and at the cinch. In the figure on the right, the colt has achieved a higher level of responsiveness. Rather than using the inside hand to show direction and encourage the colt to turn into the opened rein, use it to simply keep the colt from bending his neck as you apply the "wall" with the outside aids. To accomplish this effect, draw your inside hand to your inside hip with exactly the amount of pressure necessary to keep the colt from bending his head.

If your colt did not respond, increase the pressure until he does. Remember, do not allow your colt to bend his neck. You will not be developing shoulder control and guiding skills if you allow him or cause him to bend his neck. A slack outside rein and a strong inside rein allow the colt to bend his neck and fall out with the shoulders—a performance-hindering habit you definitely want to avoid. Again, think of your outside rein and outside leg as a creek bank or wall against which your horse bounces and is forced to change direction.

Ask for slight deviations to the right until you feel a definite improvement in the responses. Your colt will show improvement by beginning to turn as you move your outside hand in the direction of your belt buckle. At this point, the outside rein touches his neck, and he will begin to turn. Then school on turns to the left.

As your colt becomes more responsive and begins to turn at the brushing of the outside rein on his neck, use your inside reinforcing rein closer to the outside rein. In other words, rather than effect an opening rein with your inside hand, simply apply a direct rein of opposition to reinforce the neck rein. Effect a direct rein of opposition by drawing your inside hand toward your inside hip immediately above the swell of your saddle. The narrower distance between the reins is important if your horse is eventually going to guide one-handed.

Work on guiding in the same fashion until your horse responds to a light and loose outside rein with a strong deviation in the direction of travel. At this point, your colt is ready to begin guiding work on the circle. You will find it very easy to guide perfect circles on loose reins without developing the classic shoulder-out or falling out habits that are so harmful to performance.

Naturally, as you work on guiding in straight lines connected with small changes in direction, your colt learns to travel in straight lines. The ability to travel in straight lines without leaning one way or the other is a critical skill to the performance horse. Therefore, as you school on guiding and turning, you automatically school on traveling in straight

This colt responds well to the guiding aids. At the light touch of the outside rein on his neck and the outside leg at the cinch, he took a pronounced step crosswise with his outside front limb.

Here the colt takes the next step: the inside front limb reaches laterally as the shoulders move away from the outside "wall."

lines. As you ride that straight line between turns, do you feel your colt deviate to the right without your requesting the turn? Simply apply the guiding aids as if you wanted to turn the opposite way from which he is deviating and put him back on the straight line. With consistent corrections, your colt will soon learn to wait for your cues before changing direction.

The way you move your hands is important in developing and maintaining good guiding. Regardless of the stage of guiding at which your colt is performing, your hands must move slowly. The slow movement of your hands gives your colt the opportunity to feel the rein on his neck and respond correctly before you reinforce the cue with your outside leg and inside hand. That opportunity to respond before reinforcement aids are applied is critical to your colt's learning.

Also key to guiding is the fact that your outside rein hand must never cross the center of the horse's neck. Crossing the center of the horse's neck with your neck rein hand is a bad habit that results in forcing the horse's head to the outside of the turn and allowing the outside shoulder to seep under the rein or wall. Hence, the specific indication to draw your outside hand to your belt buckle when asking for the change of direction.

BACKUP

Backing up is a critical skill to the performance horse. Not only is it important for the colt to back up in order to be useful to the rider, but it is also an excellent way to firm up in the colt's mind the idea that he is to respond to light bit pressure.

Your goal in the first thirty rides is to have your colt back up to light pressure on his mouth. There should be no tossing of the head or opening of the mouth when you lift the slack

151

out of the reins for the backup. What should occur is simply a slight flexion of the poll and a consistent backup rhythm for four or five strides. Do not concern yourself if the colt backs up slightly crooked. You will fix this later once you have gained control over the hindquarters and more control over the shoulders.

To ask for the backup, lift the slack out of the reins, and create activity or motion with your legs, either by squeezing on the sides or alternately bumping on the forearms. This colt responds by backing up energetically on loose reins.

Ask for the backup by lifting the slack out of the reins and tapping your stirrups softly—first one, then the other—on the elbows or forearms. If this soft tapping creates some fear in the colt, squeeze your legs on his ribcage instead. The idea is to create a need for movement with your legs or stirrups and to close the front door with your hands. As the colt begins to respond to the impulsion that you are creating with your legs, he may simply move ahead since he does not yet know about backing up. At this moment, increase the pressure on his mouth as much as necessary to keep him from moving ahead. Keep asking with your legs. As the colt begins to step back and away from the pressure on his mouth in an effort to look for a more comfortable place to go, lighten and release the pressure on his mouth. Notice I said "as the colt begins to step back." This is critical. The more comfortable situation must happen as the colt responds, not after he has responded. This is the key to developing a colt that responds promptly to light backup cues.

As the colt responds and steps back in search of a more comfortable situation, release the pressure on his mouth and let him stand still for a few minutes. After he has stood still for one or two minutes, again lift the slack and create a need to move with your legs or stirrups. Again, let the colt stand still for a few minutes after he has backed up one step. Continue this routine of backing up one step and sitting still for a few minutes for the next twenty to thirty minutes. At this point, the colt will likely begin to back up as you lift the slack out of the reins. Or he may still need your legs or stirrups to give him some encouragement to move, but the response will come sooner and to lighter cues. He now has learned to back up.

All that is necessary to maintain a correct response to light aids is for you never to pull on his mouth and never to expect him to back up fast and several steps in a row for the next few months. Be satisfied with one, two, or three steps for backing up. Always sit still after two or three steps, and be sure that when you begin work on the backup, the exercise will last for several minutes. Backing up for several minutes, rather than backing up two or three steps and then moving forward into a different exercise, will make the backup aids very clear in your colt's mind. This clarity of purpose is critical to optimum performance.

STOPS

Your goal with regard to stops is get your colt to like stopping. You want your colt to look forward to the stop because he knows it is a comfortable place to be. You want him to think that stopping is fun and that standing still on loose reins is really something to look forward to.

To achieve this goal, you need to make sure that the right thing is more comfortable than the wrong thing. You apply this principle to the stop by making sure that your colt has plenty of time to position himself for the stop before you make the experience uncomfortable. You can also apply this principle by making sure you reward any attempt to stop. If you make sure that you respect these two objectives, your colt will stop to the best of his ability and will enjoy stopping. Both of these requirements are prerequisites to the hard stops of the cutting horse or the long, smooth, sliding stops of the cow horse and reining horse. Here is how to develop that love for the stop that leads to the great stop on a loose rein from a colt that has only been ridden thirty times.

Jog your colt until he feels like he is ready to stop. You will be able to tell by the fact that he will try to slow down even though you did not call for him to do so. At this point, ride him forward at the jog, or perhaps lope, if he is ready, for a few more minutes. By now your colt is probably breathing a bit

Saying "Whoooooa" slowly gives the colt plenty of time to get ready to stop and leads to the kind of stop Harvey Vegter gets from Darcy's Zan Parr.

heavy and really looking to stop. While on loose reins, simply say "Whooooa" slowly, and really stretch out the "o" sound. This will give your colt time to register that you are asking for something else, something different. He may try to stop based on the ground training you have given him, but he may not. If the colt stops, sit there for four or five minutes, making the right thing more comfortable than the wrong thing. If the colt ignores the word and continues to move at the regular pace, simply lift the slack out of the reins slowly, gradually increasing the pressure until he comes to a complete stop. Then immediately give the slack in the reins and sit there for four or five minutes.

At this point in the schooling program, apply your stopping aids in slow motion. This is the guarantee that your colt will like stopping. Once he likes stopping, then you can apply pressure to call for more dramatic stops. However, this will not happen for the next two or three months of consistent riding. No seesawing on the colt's mouth, no jerking the slack, and no sudden contact that causes fear and bracing are needed, simply slow-mode actions. Say the word "Whoooooa," and move your hands slowly, giving the colt plenty of time to stop without pain or pressure.

With time, your colt will begin to stop just as you start to say "Wh . . . ." You will not have to lift the slack out of the reins. He will be stopping on loose reins. This is the sign that your colt enjoys stopping. You have cracked open the door to big-time stops.

HINDQUARTER CONTROL

Hindquarter control is an integral part of the total body control that is necessary for optimum performance. Without hindquarter control, it is impossible to position the horse for correct lead transitions, turns around the barrel, stops, turning the cow on the fence, opening and closing a gate, and a host of other maneuvers we need a performance horse to execute.

Hindquarter control can be introduced to the colt as soon as he is sufficiently relaxed to move forward with relative consistency. Typically, within the first few weeks of riding, a colt is ready to begin schooling on elementary displacing leg pressure responses. In other words, when you touch your colt with your leg placed at about where the back cinch on your saddle is located, he responds by moving his hindquarters away from the pressure.

To introduce a colt to the displacing leg, ride him to the corner of a fence. The corner reduces the options the colt has for moving and makes it more obvious to him that he needs to respond by moving his hindquarters away from your leg pressure.

This response pattern is best introduced using the corner of a fence. Ride your colt until his head is well into the corner of the fence. Let him sit there for a while until he relaxes. Once he is relaxed, move one leg back on his side, about to where your back cinch is located, and press the colt's ribcage with gradually increasing pressure. If the colt responds by moving away from the pressure slightly, relax your leg and sit still for a minute or two. If he does not respond, tap with your leg until he does.

After you have stood still for a minute or two, place the same leg at the same location on the colt's ribcage, and ask for another step away from your leg. Again, reward the colt by sitting still a minute or two. Continue the one-step-per-touch-of-the-leg exercise until the colt is all the way against the far fence. Then begin by moving the colt the opposite way with your other leg.

Continue to work in the corner until the colt moves away from the position of your leg rather than from pressure. At this point, execute the exercise in the middle of the large riding area. Since the colt has a clear idea about moving his hindquarters away from the touch of your leg, it should be a simple matter to have him hold his forehand in place as he moves his hindquarters around it. This is the introduction to hindquarter control and a preparation for what comes in the next few months of schooling in the way of body control.

LOPING

So far, we have not talked about loping your colt. I have done this for two specific reasons:

1. Many riders create problems in their colt by asking him to lope too soon in the training program. In the process of applying the force of aids necessary to have the colt lope, they scare him and actually set training back rather than advancing it.

2. The more the colt responds to the aids for shoulder control, guiding, and hindquarter control, the easier it is for him to understand what you are asking for and the easier it is for you to position him so he will perform correctly the first time.

Let's discuss each of these reasons separately.

I talked about riders who lope their colts too soon. What then are the signs that the colt is ready to lope? There are a three obvious ones:

Loping relaxed and on loose reins is the result of establishing a solid foundation at the walk and jog and not rushing the colt when he breaks gait.

1. The colt jogs as soon as you ask and maintains the jog for as long as you want him to. In other words, the colt has developed rhythm and relaxation at the jog.

2. You can guide the colt anywhere you want at the jog using both hands. The changes of direction are not sharp and dramatic, but the colt is turning without bending his neck and on relatively light aids.

3. The colt gets into the stopping mode as soon as he hears you say "Whooooooa" and feels the slack lifted out of the reins.

Once your colt exhibits these three signs, loping will be a pleasant rather than scary event. In fact, it is likely that you will be able to position him so he will depart on the correct lead—a key to preventing the development of wrong lead loping.

You see, loping on the wrong lead is a sign of poor positioning of the colt's body. Poor position is the only option if you did not take the time to develop body control before you asked for the lope.

Ask for the lope the same way you asked for the jog while you where walking in the round pen. Simply reach and tap the colt on the forearm with the side of your stirrup on the outside. However, it is likely that by now you have the added bonus of having your colt respond to leg pressure on his sides, and you can simply squeeze your legs on him to have him lope.

As we said when we discussed the jog, do not expect the colt to hold the lope gait for many strides at once. If he lopes two or three strides and then breaks gait into the trot, it is fine. Let him walk on for a few strides until he is relaxed again, and then again ask for the lope. With time, the colt will gain confidence and balance and will add more strides to the lope before breaking gait.

A common mistake you must avoid is kicking the colt into the lope as soon as he breaks gait after loping two or three strides. This only scares him and gets him trotting very fast and out of balance. How can the colt be loping relaxed and in balance when he is kicked violently for breaking gait when he did not understand or keep the loping stride? Much more conducive to optimum performance is the idea of turning the break of gait into an exercise in relaxation by letting the colt walk on as if this is what you actually wanted. The result will be a colt that lopes off relaxed and maintains a slow, naturally balanced gait rather than one that rushes forward and gains speed out of fear.

AFTERWORD

Throughout this book I have described a method whereby you can develop a team relationship with your colt, one that will lead to cooperation rather than fear and resistance. I have outlined steps you can use to develop the maximum potential in your colt. I have described the signs you need to watch for as you progress through these steps and build this relationship. These signs are critical. They are the messages your horse sends your way. They are his way of communicating: sign language. Listen to your horse. Paraphrase to him what he tells you. Check the message for clarity. Respond in the appropriate, thoughtful manner. The relationship you both will enjoy will lead him to his optimum potential.

For information on Horsemanship and Horse Training Seminars designed and instructed by the author, write to:

Equine Performance Services
5413 52nd Street
Olds, Alberta, Canada T4H 1H8

INDEX